Born in Brisbane in 1920, G.... Harwood began writing poetry in her late thirties, and many of her early poems were printed in newspapers and magazines under pseudonyms such as Walter Lehmann and Miriam Stone. In 1945 she married linguist William Harwood and they moved to Tasmania where she has lived since. Her first volume, *Poems*, was published in 1963, followed by Volume Two in 1968. *The Lion's Bride* appeared in 1981, and the award-winning *Bone Scan* in 1989. Gwen Harwood has been awarded Honorary Doctorates of Letters from the Universities of Tasmania Queensland and La Trobe.

IMPRINT

The Present Tense
Gwen Harwood

Edited by Alison Hoddinott

Acknowledgement is made to the following publications in which the poems and stories first appeared:
Scripsi, Southerly, Preludes, Island, Voices, Night Thoughts (Pamphlet Poets, National Library), Ulitarra, *Luna, Endeavour, Westerly, Overland*, the *Bulletin, Riverrun, ASAE Bulletin*, the *Age Saturday Extra, Meanjin, The Tasmanian Peace Trust, Blacksmith, The Oxford Book of Australian Light Verse* and *Tilting at Matilda* (Festschrift in honour of Veronica Brady, Fremantle Arts Centre Press).

The editor, Alison Hoddinott, wishes to thank Gwen Harwood and the following people for assistance with locating the material included in *The Present Tense*: Rosemary Cohen, Stephen Edgar, Ann Jennings, Susan McMichael and Shirley Walker.

Australia Council
for the Arts

An IMPRINT book
Imprint is a division of ETT Imprint
83 Victoria St, Potts Pt, Sydney NSW 2011, Australia

First published in 1995

Distributed by
HarperCollins *Publishers*
25 Ryde Rd, Pymble, NSW 2073, Australia
31 View Rd, Glenfield, Auckland 10, NZ
HarperCollins *International*
10 East 53rd St, New York, NY 10022, USA
In de Knipscheer *Uitgeverij*
Singel 450, 1017 Av Amsterdam

ISBN 1 875892 28 1

Cover photo by Rob Gray
Cover design by Julie Allbutt, Whizzbang art, Canberra
Printed in Australia by McPherson's Printing Group

To my children

Contents

Night Thoughts   1
Herongate   2
'In Worse Armes'   4
Autumn   5
The Present Tense   7
I.M. William Hart-Smith   10
The Death of Eisenbart   11
On Uncertainty   13
Wittgenstein's Shoebox   16
Monkey Business   18
Songs of Eve I (1-9)   19
Midwinter   28
A Piece of Ivory   31

Among the Roses   33
Goddess of the Crossroads   41
Gemini   48
The Glass Boy   56

'This Artifice of Air'   66
Songs of Eve II (1-3)   70
A Gypsy Tune   73
Out of Hell   74
A Valentine   75
Later Texts (I-III)   76

Six Odes for Public Occasions
        On Poetry   79
        Little Buttercup's Picture Book   84
        On Books   90
        On History   92
        In Praise of Food   96
        Syntax of the Mind   102
A Sermon   111
'Freely they stood who stood, and fell who fell'   114
Midwinter Rainbow   125
To Music   127
Tetragrammaton   128
The Owl and the Pussycat Baudelaire Rock   134

Night Thoughts

'Hell is for those who doubt that hell exists.'
One of the elohim with whom I fight
from 4 a.m. to cockcrow, told me this.
He hit me in the thigh for emphasis.
Is it a dream? If so, the dream persists.

I meet him always at the edge of night.
He knows me, but he'll never give his name.
Why should you know, he says. I have to guess
whether he comes to punish or to bless.
I thought once he was death, but at first light

he goes, and I get up. Things are the same
as usual. The sounds of day begin:
the kettle and the news; so it's not death
who comes in the small hours to cramp my breath.
Sleep is extinguished like a candle flame.

Longing for peace I wrestle, try to pin
the adversary down. Tell me your name.
Tell me, did language lapse when mankind fell?
Tell me, is 'He descended into hell'
a metaphor? The literal truth? Where in

this universe could hell be? He persists:
'Hell is for those who doubt that hell exists.'

Herongate
(to Graeme Hetherington)

I dream I am opening the door
of Herongate lost in the fire,
gone into the world of light
in one way or another, if dreams
are as real as anything else.

In the dream the house is intact,
a world without metaphor, standing
foursquare, with its ramshackle shed
and its tanks and wreathing geraniums.
So all is well, after all,

until I look down at my hand,
at my fingers turning the key:
my bones are as white as a long-bleached shell,
as smooth, as beautiful.
I have died. It was I who died

and have come in my dream to this door,
a skeleton in a summer dress,
whose dream was fire,
whose language
must manage without any tongue
of fire, or anything else.

And what will my fingers write
without sinew or flesh, though the bones
by some strange gravitational force
that seems to be partial to dactyls
are turning my key in the lock.

O my bird-haunted shack in the dunes!
A nest that I shaped to myself.
There are streets I can't cross for the ghosts,
but in Paradise nothing can happen.
Alone, I invested in silence,

except for the resident possums.
I hope they escaped from the fire.
This hope marks the edge of my dream
as I wake in the city, alive.
Far off, a faint bloom in the marshes

is announcing a change of season,
and perhaps an invisible presence
that does not startle the herons
cries out by the desolate tankstands
to purge its grief, is waiting

like a satyr straight out of Isaiah
with the cormorant and the bittern
possessing the stones of emptiness
until I return, to tell me
my days will not be prolonged.

'In Worse Armes'

The shell of Cancer Magister
(so I read in a book) will fit
exactly in the Golden Rectangle.
Remembering this, I told myself
all shall be well, all shall be well,
the day I got the diagnosis.

Death took me off for questioning
and then released me. 'What you hear
is not what you will hear. Beethoven
when he was working used to thump
the lower keys with his left hand
to hide what his right hand was playing.'

Autumn

To the memory of Vincent Buckley

Once in Melbourne, billeted
in a lecturer's room at Ormond,
I answered the phone expecting
a call from you, and breathed,
con amore, Irish Darling.
A startled professor replied
'I seem to have got the wrong room.'

An earlier winter night
in Hobart: my children show you
their treasures, shells, fossils, a scale
model of Stonehenge in balsa.
One gives you a lecture on Druids
while I get the dinner, find pencils,
check schoolbags, rehearse the homework.

I Mother, you in the haze
of your academic glory.
younger than I, and sadder
than I have ever been,
we talk when the house is quiet.
I remember your saying, 'Happiness
precludes the greatest joy.'

Nearly thirty years on I am sitting
playing Scrabble with your young daughters.

One gives me a lecture on guineapigs
while your wife is getting the dinner.
Our last day on earth together.
Grania waits through the game
to put down her one word: Ireland.

Some say that primates evolved
concurrently with fruit trees;
we passed them on, they gave us
our colour vision, our taste for sweetness.
What gave us our salty rapture then
at a cry from the stage: It is no matter now
who lives or who dies.

What's metaphor to me.
or nature playing at theatre.
Let autumn repeating its moral office
of ripeness, let its adorning
be blown away, away.
Things pile up, a heap of crutches:
the must-be-done. Props for the living.

Rake, pruning shears, a fire
of dry leaves gilded with death.
'More and more of the immortals
were dying,' you wrote. I was charmed
by your presence in the world
to distraction. The day is far spent,
Irish Darling. It's mortals who die.

The Present Tense
I. M. Vincent Buckley

'What does it mean to move
out of the present tense?'
I asked you in a dream
not long after your death.
You said, 'We live two lives.
One in the world, and one
in what others write about us.'
In the dream it was towards evening.

As many suns in the galaxy
as nerve cells in the brain.
My skull's a dome of darkness,
the only room of my own
I'll have this side of death.

Today's the feast of Corpus Christi.
Honey out of the rock. The sun
after a moment's elevation
is veiled in a Bridgewater Jerry.
Seagulls head for the tip. My blackbird
takes his life in his throat. The sparrows
come close for crumbs. Is this a world
containing in itself all hunger?

Pain's your continuing absence from the world
among other matters.
                    'Love is not a feeling.
              Why is pain not put to the test like love?
              If it were true pain, would it go away?'
Who said such things? Saint Ludwig of Vienna.
That thinker should have used the Queensland *but*.
Love's not a feeling, but. Real pain is not
put to the test, but. Doesn't sound so pompous.
A difficult man, one much in need of friendship.
A genius. Didn't like women, but.
Thank God you did. It was beatitude
to talk shop to a man who plainly liked me.
You'd met the doctor who nursed Wittgenstein.

              The bells of Holy Trinity
              call the living. Foursquare, massive,
              crowned with spirelets, Blackburn's tower
              is silhouetted on rolling mist.
              Great bells have jostling overtones
              containing, Leonardo thought,
              the timbre of all human voices.
              Where's yours? The crescent honeyeater
              offers a senseless answer: EGYPT.

This north-east facing cottage suits
one with four-in-the-morning horrors.
I'm always up to see the sunrise,
know where the sun is when it's cloudy.

One of my children built Stonehenge in balsa
as it was when it was new, in perfect scale.
On the first night we ever ate together
he showed you how the stones were oriented,
and where the sun rose on midsummer morning.
'There was human sacrifice,' he said with relish.

Tired after our gentle-hearted
walk by the billabong, you went
homeward by car, and when we parted
I walked back slowly, thinking over
our discourse, with the firm intent
of fixing in my head forever,

as in a painting, the spring light
of happiness on children chasing
their happy dogs, the Sunday-bright
families and the brilliant blue
parrots feeding in grass; clouds racing
shadows fleeting as thought. I drew

near to your house. A man was sitting
on a low garden wall, outlined
in evening light, his body fitting
itself to age and pain. He heard
my footstep, rose and smiled. We twined
arms, and walked on without a word.

I.M. William Hart-Smith

I thought somehow some day I'd meet you
on the circuit, at a festival, at some time—
the world being round. We met in fact
only in the index of anthologies
with Harpur, Harris, Hart, Haskell and Hasluck,
or not even there if either of us should be missing
between Lesbia Harford and (roughly) Dorothy
                        Hewett.
You wrote about things I like. I should have written
to tell you I think The Ship's Cat is a knockout.

What a day to die, Easter Sunday, with death's
                        dominion ended,
and you gone to immeasurable remoteness.
Your words beat back to my mind
and melt once more to poems.

The Death of Eisenbart

He dreams of what Ouspensky saw
in Poland before World War One:
two heavy lorries with their load
of new unpainted wooden crutches
reaching up to the first floor windows

for legs which were not yet torn off.

I was responsible. Absurd.
I was at school just starting Latin
and fencing. Even then I thought
of games which had not been invented
at which I'd shine. He calls the nurse

she's reminiscent of his mistress
when he first took her, long ago.
He tells her 'You belong to me.'
Then says, 'Forgive me. I have thoughts
that have no business in my head.'

In pain, he has a premonition
of what his real pain will be;
so few good memories preserved.
His porridge comes. The young nurse feeds him
and tidies him, and combs his beard,

11

and he recalls his mistress packing
cumquats in jars of heavy syrup.
Let living things be kept, one thought
of warmth on a grey afternoon.
A clergyman comes in. He carries

a neat black briefcase edged with chrome.
Eisenbart, as the lid is lifted,
says loudly 'Sweet old Whistling Jesus!'
— 'Do you still have the power to curse?'
he asks the clergymen politely.

The wardsmaid brings a get-well card:
a fat koala wearing braces
to keep its rompers up, the sky
thick with balloons. Wrong room, she says,
taking it back. It's not for him.

What is? More pain. A taste of chaos.
'Listen to me,' he tells the nurse,
who changes, as the drugs take hold,
to his young mistress, 'Facts alone
are able to express a sense.'*

Someone on crutches, in clear moonlight,
seems to approach. Or is he moving
out of this putty-coloured room
where any name he had means nothing?
Listen, he says, as he dies, frowning.

*[Nur Tatsachen können einen Sinn ausdrücken.]

On Uncertainty

'Why can we not teach a cat to retrieve? Does it not
understand what we require of it?' — Wittgenstein

We all know that Yeats was silly
like us; but Wittgenstein was sillier
and really not like us at all.
He said himself he wrote for men
who'd breathe, one day, a different air.
In that case, they'd need different lungs.
Never rely on metaphor.

I see him as a gifted poet
who somehow never found his way
to writing poems. 'A poem can pierce us,'
he wrote. Also, 'A poem is not
used in the language game of giving
information.'
                                What you see
as the sun sets is not the sun:

that's down below the earth's horizon.
You see an image of the sun
refracted through earth's atmosphere.
Some poems that look as clear as air
carry an image of what's gone.

Fade like a smiling Cheshire Cat,
you orb of day! You cats, come out!

You never stumble in the dark.
Beware of Faithful Fido, fouling
the footpaths, waiting to retrieve
his master's footwear. Fido knows
what is required of him: his soul.
They say that Wittgenstein was handsome
as Lucifer before the fall.

His gestures linger. Old disciples
still screw their faces up like him.
Students of students use his tones
of voice. What made him think of cats?
It's not known that he ever had one.
Perhaps he did, and tried to teach it,
and came to grief (his usual state).

Perhaps, unwilling to admit
defeat, he thought the cat was stupid
(as were most people that he met).
Perhaps it turned its back on him
as he would turn his back on people.
It would have done him good to own one,
to sit and watch the sun set, stroking

a creature quite indifferent
to human guilt, for whom the riddle
did not exist. He might have felt

14

his tension crackle off and vanish,
and spared his colleagues suicidal
Austro-Hungarian-Empire grapplings
with things that never were the case.

I've read of an old chimpanzee
to whom researchers taught sign language.
He grew, not unsurprisingly,
to loathe his captors, so they shipped him
off to a zoo in San Diego
where, an Ape-Ovid in exile,
he tried to teach his fellow captives.

'If we could teach a lion to speak
how could we hope to understand it?'
That's Wittgenstein again. If only
he'd kept a cat, like Dr Johnson,
and held it in his lap, and brushed it,
and really listened to its purring,
he might have been a happier man.

Wittgenstein's Shoebox

Tell me, ye powers that dwell below,
how did this shoebox come to be
on a stall in Salamanca market?

Are they philosophers approaching?
No, clergymen. I needn't worry.
Fifty cents, and it's mine for ever.

The box is crammed with paper slips:
mixed-up observations, thoughts
on the origins of human language.

> Think of a language where each word
> is used and understood once only.
> Leaf-drift of useless syllables!

> If a cane toad could be taught to speak
> how could we know if it were lying?
> Think of the neural infrastructure.

Here's the man himself. He wants his box back.
'Ludwig—' He scowls. 'Herr Wittgenstein,
has the verb *to dream* a present tense?'

I tell him, 'Once I saw a raven
eating chips from a paper bag
on a high branch of this very plane tree.

'Corvus tasmanicus. Believe me.'
He doesn't, and the paper strips
fly up and deck the tree with leaves.

I wake, as always, with my problems
unsolved. It's true about the raven.
I can bring you a living witness.

Monkey Business

They took some newborn chimpanzees —
no, let us use the passive voice —
the newborn chimpanzees were taken
and tested in experiments.
Some were raised in total darkness;
some (in quite recent repetitions)
were brought up in unpatterned light.

A bowl of milky glass positioned
over their heads excluded patterns,
but let the baby chimps see light.
Released into the normal world
after two months, with patterned fields
available, the groups were found
in each case functionally blind.

Environmental deprivation,
we learn, changes the nervous system.
Well, we must all love one another
or die. I wish those pliant creatures
whose polypeptide sequences
are 99% like ours
could do some evil in return.

Songs of Eve I

1

Master of chaos, hold me close.
A voice clears darkness from pure space.

Fondle me. I am someone's name,
A form the world has never known.

A cracking dream. My bones are making,
one, and another. Light is breaking.

2

Cold sheets of colour, fingernail
of heavenly body, naked man,
clothed deity. And I begin
to know myself more beautiful

than all God's bright and simple shapes,
and feel the dews of passion ease
the lock of my unopened thighs,
see light possess earth's gentle slopes,

Adam's wide-open ribcage spring,
across a pulsing darkness, shut.
Bone of my bone, I know without
remembering, I speak your tongue.

3

Adam, what have you there?
It is a small bird, surely,
hatched out of God's blue breathing.
I feel it in my hand
trembling in warmth, and rising,
defying the grave earth
with its strange wings, grossly mounted.
My winged love, my soaring bliss.

4

So this is the best
of all possible worlds.
His cleansing wit ordained it so:

the thrust and rapture
ordained to fall
back into ocean's shimmering witness.

The cock in full brilliance
crowing up morning,
body illumined and spirit touching

horizons alight
with a tinge of madness,
the afterglow of a lunatic moonset.

Eye to mind
in a raging welcome
we lie beyond the kingdom of darkness.

He leaves us alone
to paint our sensations
our fairy tales, our fiery tales.

It is I, it is you,
in a crown of gold feathers
soaring and singing.

5

Angelo Draco, travelling salesman,
knocked at the door. Asked for my husband.

      'Representing, *The Fruit of Knowledge*.
      Think how the set would look on your shelf.

      My product will help you to get ahead.
      win scholarships, make the best of yourself.

      Let me summarise, in case I've confused you,
      we publish a year-book every year.

      Eight, ten, twenty years into the future
      we'll still be in touch with you. Sign here.'

6

Blood drop by blood
      drop by drop
            by drop
And the kingfisher takes me
      to his rank nest,
           warm food for his children,
In the smell of old fish and leaves and mould
a murderous demon not yet revealed
rejoices that God has wounded me.
Infants a handspan long are crawling
damnation-mad on the floor of hell.
Adam is hunting, his hounds are singing,
the deer is stricken. God creates nothing.
The world exists from eternity.

7

I had no childhood, but
      my daughters will be children.

I have no mother, but
      my children will be daughters.

It needs no cosmic wrong,
   only the puzzled, growing
      wretchedness of one child,
         blind, whose friend says: 'Look!'

Adam as Black Minstrel, Eve as Mammy

'Tarbaby, tarbaby, hush your cryin'
the stars are swarmin' the sunset's dyin'.
   Hush your mouf, girl, spade's a spade.
   I'm gonna get our firstborn laid.'

Who's gonna lay him? Things is grim.
There's only me and you and him.

'You want your boy to be a fairy?
Read your Bible Commentary:

Keep on readin' and shut your face.
We're all symbols of the human race.

Shine your shoes, boy, time to go
off to the whorehouse with Daddy-o.'

   'Daddy I can't make it in this heathen place.
   All of those whores have my Mammy's face.'

Tune: The House of the Rising Sun

All seasons through all centuries
        as mistress, whore and wife,
my body like a hollow reed
        has shaped the sound of life.

Philosophers and Saints have breathed
        their wisdom in my bed.
King David sleeps beside his harp.
        Great Solomon is dead.

My daughters grind the bones of kings
        in fields where armies bled
to nourish the immortal wheat
        to make their children's bread.

My soul dares to reveal itself
        now God himself is dead.
Old earth will give her yielding seed
        to see my daughters fed.

Midwinter

Midwinter, and the treasures of the snow
fall as chill rain on Salamanca Market.
A day for a good book, and here's a bargain:
a commentary on the Book of Job.
Queensland Book Depot, Albert Street. O Brisbane

have you sent me this text, and to what end,
from my old lunch-hour haunt, how have you found me?
Speak, memory: a red-haired child is sitting
beside her grandmother, who's busy sewing
braid on her son-in-law's Masonic apron.

I'd heard about my father's God, the Great
Architect of the Universe, a being
served by his menfolk in their fancy aprons.
My mother's God rode on her hip, the boy-child
to whom she sang, at whom she smiled all day.

My father's house: a small War Service cottage,
verandas back and front, a fruitful acre
with horse, cow, ducks and fowls, an orange orchard,
a neat path leading through the fenced-off peas.
'A path,' my father grinned, 'which no fowl knoweth.'

'Read to me, my dear.' I want my comics,
but Tiger Tim and Jolly Joking Jumbo
will have to wait. The place is marked in Job.
Gold, crystal, sapphire, onyx, topaz, rubies—
I know the jewels by heart, but wisdom's better.

My grandmother was born in eighteen-eighty.
Married at seventeen and widowed early
she loved her native Queensland, and the future
in the shadow of God's hand did not confound her
in a world where good and evil grew together.

She used one text as if it were a charm:
'Though he slay me, yet will I trust in him.'
I see that's an inspired mistranslation
of He will slay me. I will wait for him.
Lo, he will kill me, and I will not hope.

I will be slain, but with my face towards him.
Is that why we like games? Who'd go to matches
if the full forwards lay down? Wrestle with angels!
Now at three-score and ten, I seem to live
most of the time in existential terror.

I think of Hume, modest philosopher,
approaching death 'composed in mind, and free
from anxiety, impatience or low spirits,'
and of my grandmother (who'd never read him)
accepting age and illness in that spirit.

One a great sceptic, one a true believer.
He'd have liked her He took particular pleasure
in the company, he said, of modest women.
When Job is questioned, snow is ranked with death,
with the morning stars, and lightning, and Leviathan.

Snow settles on the mountain as I read.
If death prove an experience I live through,
good angel, guide me to a sunlit kitchen
with bread rising, the great black kettle singing
of wisdom and the peaceful life to come.

A Piece of Ivory

I would grieve over fallen finches,
drowned frogs, an occasional duckling
that did not live to be eaten,
but this was beyond me.
At bedtime
my father said 'You remember
the circus you saw at Enoggera?
Well, one of the elephants went mad
and killed a keeper who used to torment it.'

'And serve him right', my grandmother said.

My father continued 'It had to be shot
They made the other elephants dig it a grave
in the paddock, and help to bury it.'

I saw them in wrinkled twilight
swaying with spades in their trunks,
chained one to another, crying
and digging a grave for their friend.

Next morning, unroofing the graves
of Finch, Frog, Duck, I ran howling
at what gave shine to the world
then took it away forever.

I remember my grandmother's comfort,
my being allowed to play
with her particular treasure:
an enamelled Indian casket
full of handcarved ivory elephants,
diminishing, the smallest
the size of a grain of wheat.
But carved. The artist cared.

Among the Roses

In one of my Christmas annuals was a spell to make fairies visible. It began

Take a wizened child of seven,
Take her from the smoky street,
Let her see the light of heaven
On a field of golden wheat.

I considered myself thin enough to be wizened. The pale dust stirred in our long street like smoke. I stood among the sweet corn, but the spell never worked. Sometimes my father said teasingly 'I know where you can see a couple of old fairies'. This made my mother laugh and my grandmother frown. 'That will do,' she would say, 'that will *do*.

One morning when my mother had taken the Little Man with her in the sulky to visit friends, my grandmother and I were preparing for a baking day in the kitchen. We heard someone running round the house to the back steps, and went out to the back verandah. Mr Snoad stood on the steps holding the rail, gasping and crying. Rivers of tears ran down through his powder and rouge.

33

'Please come quickly.' he said to my grandmother. 'Mr Mandl is bleeding to death. Please come, please.'

'The clean rag-bag, quickly!'

As I ran to get it I heard Mr Snoad say, 'The little girl...there's such a lot of blood.'

'She'll be all right. Blood doesn't worry her.'

That was true. I came from a family of nose-bleeders. It did us good. We would never have high blood-pressure. The teacher in second babies fainted the first time my nose bled in her class. A boy whose mother was a nurse removed the arum lilies from a vase and poured water over the teacher. His friend was about to empty the tadpole jar when she revived. The headmaster sent her to lie down, and entertained us by writing our names in illuminated letters on the board, using a whole virgin box of coloured chalks.

I had never been inside the house where Mr Snoad and Mr Mandl lived. Their weatherboard cottage was close to the street in front. High fences and trellises hid their back garden, which ran through a double allotment to the street behind. Delicious flower scents always hung in the air. One of the Bowers boys, who climbed in and was savagely bitten by a small prancing fox terrier that sometimes snarled through the gate, said the dog had got out; but my friend Alice told on him and he got a whipping from his mother as well as a dog bite.

Mr Snoad, still sobbing, took us in through the front door, through a cool dark passage and into a bedroom where Mr Mandl lay, apparently lifeless, in

34

a black-painted and brass-knobbed double bed.

'Oh, it's only his *nose*,' said my grandmother. She leaned over and seized Mr Mandl's large nose firmly, holding the nostrils tight with her thumb and forefinger.

Mr Mandl breathed in gasps through his mouth and moaned, but my grandmother held on for several minutes. 'There you are,' she said, finally letting go. 'It will have stopped.' Mr Snoad clung to the bedstead, pale and fainting.

'Where's the kitchen? Come along, I'll make you a hot drink. Gwennie will stay with Mr Mandl and tell me if his nose starts again.'

She led the collapsing Mr Snoad away and I watched Mr Mandl recovering among a heap of gory white towels and handkerchiefs.

'My flannel, please,' whispered Mr Mandl.

I brought his face flannel from the white-tiled washstand, which had enchanting frilly curtains of its own, hung from a carved frame above the marble. Mr Mandl cleaned his face and smiled bravely.

'Why does your washstand have curtains?'

'To catch the splashes, I suppose.'

I gathered up the linen into a bundle, and offered Mr Mandl a clean rag, which he tucked into his pyjama pocket.

'What does M.M.M stand for,' I asked, pointing to the monogram,'do all your names start with M?'

'Ah, yes, my dear: Manfred Maximilian Mandl. But Mr Snoad calls me Freddy.'

His nose seemed to have stopped for good, so I took the bundle of linen and went down the passage and through the back door to look for the troughs. The wash-house was in an open shed, wreathed in climbing roses which even poked through gaps in the boards. I knew what to do: rinse, soak, rinse, rub the bloodstains with soap, roll up, leave in cold water. The bluebag was too tempting, and I coloured the last water, which had lost all traces of carmine, deeper and deeper blue.

'You know I told you to stay with Mr Mandl.'

'I'm sorry, Granny. I was soaking the towels.'

'That's a good girl, but you shouldn't have used the bluebag. Go back to Mr Mandl.'

Mr Mandl seemed well enough to talk to. I was in the middle of a story about how pennies were made, which I had just read in my Children's Encyclopaedia, when my grandmother carried in a tray.

'Mr Snoad is still very upset,' she said. 'I will stay with him. You look after Mr Mandl. Pour carefully. Don't spill on the traycloth.'

She had made delicate rolls of crustless thin brown bread and put out some almond biscuits. I saw with greedy relief that she had provided for two. The teacups were so fine you could see the light through them. Now that the excitement was over I could stare around the room. Plate glass mirrors on the doors of a splendid wardrobe reflected Mr Mandl through the bars of his bed; he looked like the genial honey-bear in my animal book, smiling in his cage.

In a corner a set of shelves bore his treasures: a tankard, an opalescent vase, some small glass ornaments not meant for careless hands like mine. Roses rubbed against the window-glass.

'Lots of sugar,' said Mr Mandl. 'And just a dash of milk please. Oh I am relieved. Mr Snoad thought I would bleed to death. Help yourself to the food. Do you know what Mandl means? It means an almond. Have a Mandl biscuit, my dear!'

We both thought this was very funny. He looked at us in the wardrobe mirror.

'My hair is silver and yours is ginger. But we both have brown eyes, nut-brown. Do you know what your Granny is?'

At once I became uneasy. Was this someone planning to take my grandmother away?

'She's a widow,' I replied.

'Oh no,' said Mr Mandl. 'She's an *angel*.'

'Where do you keep your cow?'

'We don't have a cow, my dear. We put out a billy.'

'Do any ladies live in your house?'

'Goodness me, no. Mr Snoad and I manage very well. He does the house, and I do the garden.'

This seemed to fit. Mr Snoad was pale, and Mr Mandl golden-brown.

'We're very different,' he continued. 'I like to get up very late, and he likes to get up very early. I like to smoke, and he hates cigarettes. I have to smoke in the garden. I'm untidy, he's tidy. I like to do the shopping, he likes to stay inside.'

He told me an exciting story of escape from his enemies in disguise; of a journey on the longest railway in the world, of travelling from China on a boat and meeting Mr Snoad who was very seasick and lonely; of their finding just the right place in the world to settle down in peace and quiet, with lovely chocolate soil for the roses.

I recited a poem I knew by heart:

> The prisoner sun, in his cloud-tower throws
> A silver ladder from sky to land.
> A breeze as soft as a gentle hand
> Brushes the cheek of each rain-drenched rose.

Mr Mandl thought it very beautiful.

'I'd like to give you a little present, if your Granny says I may. Do you know what a pagoda is?'

Yes, I had read about pagodas, and I told him all I knew about pagodas and a great many other things. He listened patiently, then asked me to bring him the piece of deep blue glass from the corner shelf. He held it up to the light.

'There now, can you see it? Look in the glass, and tell me what you see. It's a kind of magic, really.'

I turned the glass obelisk, and a shining pagoda appeared; I turned the glass again, and it was gone.

My grandmother came to get the teatray.

'Be careful with that ornament.'

'Granny, Mr Mandl says I may keep it.'

'That's very kind, but you know you shouldn't ask for things.'

'It was my offer,' said Mr Mandl. 'It would give me great pleasure if you would accept a small gift for your household.'

'*Please*,' said Mr Snoad, appearing at the door. He had washed his face, but still looked like a rain-drenched rose. '*Please*, I don't know what we should have done without you. And you've even seen to the linen.'

'It's a magic glass,' I said. 'I promise not to break it.'

If you have any trouble with the stains,' said my grandmother briskly to Mr Snoad, 'collect the wood ashes from the stove. Put a clean rag over the linen, then pour boiling water over the ashes and leave the things to soak for an hour. The potash will make them perfectly white. Remember, pinching the nose hard stops the bleeding. Now, you promised me some cuttings.'

'I'll put Frisky on his chain. He doesn't *mean* to bite, but he gets excited.'

'Foxies are great little nippers,' said my grandmother.

I feared all dogs, and decided to stay inside with Mr Mandl and the glass obelisk. While I was telling him some Tales from Shakespeare he fell asleep. Mr Snoad tiptoed in and covered him tenderly with the white counterpane. My grandmother, holding a brown-paper sheaf of cuttings, beckoned to me. I did not dare to ask about the glass ornament, but picked up our clean rag-bag and followed her home.

That evening, my grandmother was telling my mother about her visit. 'The house is spotless, and the roses—I've never seen such roses—'

My father arrived home with a small parcel.

'Extraordinary thing,' he said. 'Old Snoad has never spoken to me in his life. Runs inside if he sees me. But tonight he came to the gate and gave me this. Said to tell you Mandl sent it.'

'Maybe the old anarchist has put a bomb in it,' said my mother.

But Granny and I knew what it was. 'Just a trinket,' she said, 'a souvenir for Gwennie.'

'All that fuss over a nosebleed,' said my mother.

It was too dark for the magic pagoda to shine when I was tucked in that night, but I put it under my pillow to wait for the light of heaven in the morning.

Goddess of the Crossroads

My father had a joke about me which made visitors laugh, though I did not understand it. 'We call her Salonola, the only non-scratch talking machine on the market.' By remaining neither heard nor seen while my mother and grandmother chatted to their friends from town, I had learned my character, and took great interest in it. I could talk the leg off an iron pot; I ate everything, but you could never fill me up or put an ounce of meat on me; I could read anything; you would not know I was listening, but afterwards I could repeat things word for word; my nose had been put out of joint when the Little Man was born; I was terrified of the dark.

No doubt our visitors found other and shorter descriptions of me to enliven their train journey home: a talkative, greedy, jealous, skinny little nosey-parker. I was certainly terrified of the dark. Having learned to pray at Sunday School, I prayed, standing at my bedroom window, to the fairies. Sometimes I saw them moth-pale and wavering in the grasses. I asked them to let me live forever, and to take away the baby and leave in his place a changeling, preferably a hedgehog or a small red fox. Imagine my mother's surprise when she looked in the basket-weave hamper! By day things were substantially themselves, trustworthy, but at night they changed. I did not believe my teacher when she said that darkness was not a thing, but just the absence of light: when we called the roll each child would answer 'Present' to his name; but if he were not there, she would write 'Absent'. It was like that, she said. The light was simply away. The children knew better. Darkness, like the word 'Absent' written in red ink, was something.

We had a country girl called Grace to help in the afternoons. By the time I returned from school she would have hung out the baby's washing while my mother had her rest and my grandmother crocheted intricate fine cloths or worked glittering bead flowers on velvet. Grace would take my school bag and tidy away the papers and the white napkin in which my sandwiches were wrapped; she would rinse and set to dry the sponge from the sponge-tin, and wash the smeary slate. My four-o-clock would be set out: a thick slice of home-made bread and butter with Windsor sausage, which my grandmother called German sausage. I did not like this name for it. I knew all about the Germans, the Huns, the gorilla-like monsters who threatened women and children in kitchens like ours; under the house in a trunk thought safe from my fingers were the Norman Lindsay posters at which I loved to look in daylight.

When they came at night, step by evil step through the shadows, I would say the magic word: Gallipoli, Gallipoli, as I covered my head.

But it was afternoon, and the misery of school was over, and I was back in paradise with my orange taken from the box of dry-creek-sand. I should have loved to eat it slowly on our walk, as Grace pushed the baby and I hung on the handle of the pram talking, talking, talking. But eating in the street was utterly forbidden; so was going into people's houses, or going to the creek. Grace was one of a large, honest, sober, industrious family who lived up the road from us; I understood that she was a country girl from a way my mother, essentially urban, had of saying 'She's only been to town *twice* in her *life*.' We would wave to Grace's mother, who was almost always washing, poking at clothes in the outdoor copper with a huge bleached copper-stick, or gathering them in, but she would not come to the gate to see the Little Man as so many women did; she had seen enough of them. At the dusty crossroads we could go right, or left, but not onwards to the creek. One day we stopped by a small flaking white weatherboard house near the crossroads. Black fowls picked and scratched among the ferns and roses. I said loudly to Grace, 'A witch lives here.' I believed it. My mother called the old woman who lived there 'The Gypsy'. My father referred to her as 'The old witch'. I had never seen her closely, but my friend Alice said that she looked like an owl, and had a chopper.

'Don't be silly,' said Grace. 'She's a fortune-teller. She told me my fortune, and said I would be rich one day.' The Little Man, because his pram had stopped moving, started to howl. Grace rocked the pram and tickled him, but he howled more loudly. The old woman appeared at her gate.

I drew away, afraid, but she walked slowly towards me and put a hand on my head. 'What splendid hair!' She stroked me like an animal. Then she turned to the pram and lifted my brother in his frilly clothes high in the air, as my father loved to do. He stopped crying, and she gave him to Grace.

'Come inside, out of the sun. You are all much too hot.' And so, it seemed, we had been, when we sat on her cool verandah shaded by green canvas blinds. She poured a mug of water from the stone water-monkey and we looked at one another as I drank. She did indeed look like an owl with her round goldrimmed glasses and feathery white hair. 'Tell me my fortune again,' said Grace.

The old woman shook her head. She kept staring at me. 'So unlike the mother,' she said, and to Grace, 'I read the mother's hand. I told her she would have the boy.'

I read the mother's hand. Were hands, then, like books?

'Give me your hand, child.'

I put down the thick china mug of cold water on a wicker table and she turned my hands gently in hers. 'A good hand,' she said. 'A lucky hand.' She drew her finger across one palm. 'A long life, like the mother.' Her soft touch and tender strange voice held me captive as an animal that knows it cannot escape and must keep as still as death. The baby sat quietly on Grace's knee.

From a shelf the old woman took a pack of playing cards. For a moment I thought we were all going to play 'Snap', or 'Strip-Jack-Naked', but she knelt on the wooden verandah boards and began to arrange the cards in front of me in a semi-circle, in groups of three, murmuring over and over, 'Bombo, Mormo, Yellow Capella, Bombo, Mormo, Yellow Capella.' She told my fortune in the same soothing voice, looking up at me now and again with her owl-eyes, but I can remember nothing of it except the promise of four children.

She put the cards away and said, 'Off you go now. Back home.'

Off we went, a fourteen-year-old, a rogue from First Babies, and a real baby. At home again I was uncontrollably wild and naughty, and my mother sent me to play in the garden while Grace prepared the vegetables and my grandmother went to do the milking, remarking that Satan had got into me. She meant it literally. When everyone thought I was with someone else I slipped through the post and rail fence and started off for the forbidden creek. Since I had transgressed by *going into someone's house* and had not been punished I thought myself invulnerable. I walked quickly past the crossroad and on

45

through the lantana patches to the place where the men and boys swam on Saturday afternoons, a rocky basin under the shade of the ironbarks.

The creek, empty of human beings, seemed oddly sinister. The voices of water did not suggest I was welcome. I longed to run home, but was determined to enjoy myself. Sometimes, when I refused to give in, or admit I was wrong, my father would recite

O the queen is proud on her throne,
And proud are her maids so fine,
But the proudest lady that ever was known
Is this little lady of mine.

I said the verse to myself to give me courage. I leaned over the bank to look at my reflection, saw only shadow, and slipped down on to a rock, cutting my knee. The swift twilight began. The bank loomed above me, to an adult a stretching step, to me a fearful height. Who would help me? *What* would come? Gallipoli! Gallipoli!

The old woman, the gypsy, the witch. No doubt she had seen me from her garden, and followed. But she appeared like a miracle, hauled me up the steep bank, and, without a word, held me tightly for a moment.

I ran home, and, sneaking through the side fence, saw Grace leaving and my father arriving at the front gate. Under his protection I went in and sat with my bleeding knee hidden by the table.

My grandmother was setting out the breathing lamps.

My father got the cards from the drawer and said, 'How about a game of snap before tea?'

I said, 'I'll tell your fortune,' and began putting the cards out in a semicircle, reciting 'Bombo, Mormo, Yellow Capella, Bombo, Mormo, Yellow Capella.' I told him he would be rich and live for ever.

My grandmother said sharply, 'Where did you learn such things? What have you been doing? Where have you been?'

But my mother said, 'Leave her alone; she's only playing.'

I read the mother's hand.

Mother, you are like an old gypsy yourself now with your snowy hair and tanned skin; the promise of long life was true, and I have had my four children, and will have my long life. I alone can remember you as you stood by my bed, young and beautiful, chasing away my nightmares with lamplight. 'There is nothing to be afraid of.' Now it is I who must comfort you against the dark.

Gemini

'Go down and skim the cream,' said my grand-
mother. 'We are to have visitors.' I took the cream jug
carefully. On one side of it were the heads of Jellicoe,
Kitchener and Haig and some words which I knew by
heart:

> *Come the three corners of the world in arms,*
> *And we shall shock them. Nought shall make*
> > *us rue,*
> *If England to itself do rest but true.*

On the other side was a painting of a pink rose.
As I stood on the box skimming the cream I thought of
what Georgy Bowers had said when he caught me at
the gate. When school began again next week he and
his brother were going to throw my port in the creek
and drown me. I had kept close to my grandmother all
morning.

As I carried the cream upstairs the Hudson Super
Six drew up at the front gate. The Doctor and the
twins got out and walked round to the back verandah,
as friends always did. The twins had golden-brown
skin and dark curly hair. Their real names were Otmar

and Annie, but they called themselves Otto and Anna. 'We prefer palindromes,' Otto had told me. I thought them the most beautiful people in the world, and wrote 'palindrome' and 'lustrous' in my book of words that evening. My grandmother said I should write in 'besotted' and 'infatuated', but I did not like those words.

My friend Alice was not allowed to play with the twins. Her mother told my mother that she woke up wet and screaming after their games. They did not go to the State School, where the big boys had undressed them on their first day to see if twins were any different, but were taught in the mornings by a retired schoolmistress. In the afternoons they did what they liked until their father came home. Was he a real doctor? He had a clinic in town for the Diagnosis and Treatment of All Chronic Diseases. He was as golden-brown as the twins, as plump as they were thin. Their mother had died at their birth. 'We were brought up by fallen girls from the Good Shepherd,' Anna had told my shocked grandmother one day. But my father said it was a good idea. 'You know they're clean if the Sisters of Mercy have had them.'

On the table were cold duck, cold peas and salad, home-made bread and butter, fruit salad and my jug of cream. 'What a feast,' said the Doctor. A feast! I longed for butcher's meat, shop bread and butter and bought cakes. But we could not have meat until we had eaten the last of the old ducks, and Daisy was still giving three gallons. While we ate, the Doctor kept praising my grandmother's cooking and saying things like 'You're wasted here,' and 'You really should have a household of your own.' I was not allowed to speak at table unless spoken to. When the Doctor finally spoke to me he said, 'How would you feel if I took your Granny away with me?'

Fear made me silly. I shouted, 'I'd stab you, I'd cut you, I'd poison you, I'd kill you.' I was slapped and made to say I was sorry. The twins, whose manners were always perfect, went on eating.

'Perhaps you had better go and play at the twins' place. The Doctor and I have to talk to one another.'

We cleared and stacked the dishes, and my grandmother gave us an orange each. 'Don't eat in the street, don't take your shoes off. When you hear the train, go to the gate and come home with your mother.' The twins were all charm. 'We'll take care of her. Thank you for the lovely dinner. How pretty your hair looks with the big comb in. We adore home-made butter. Some day will you teach up to make bead mats? Can we give you a goodbye kiss?'

As soon as we were out of the gate the twins began peeling and eating their oranges. They sat down and took off their shoes and socks and walked in the soft white dust at the edge of the road. 'We're not afraid of your Granny,' said Otto. I was worried. 'If my Granny married your father, would she be your Granny too?' 'Good heavens, no,' said Anna. 'She'd be our step-mother.' 'And what would my mother be?'

Nobody could work out the complications. 'Are you afraid of God?' I asked.

'God is just a word,' said Anna.

Mrs Chatband waved her three fingers at us. Her son had left a razorblade in his school trousers on washing day. So many terrible edges in the world! My friend Alice was on her front verandah playing school with her dolls. The dolls were lined up with their knickers down, waiting to be caned.

In the front yard of the Bowers place Georgy and Davey were skinning frogs. Two frogs waiting their turn were impaled on wooden meat skewers, still moving feebly. Georgy lifted his knife towards me and said quietly, 'We'll get you.' The twins, who had been walking on either side of me, said 'Run!'. We ran to the safety of their gate. They dropped their shoes and the remains of their oranges and put their arms around me. I did not quite come up to their shoulders. 'How old are you now?' asked Otto. 'Seven.' 'Don't be afraid. We will teach you the words of revenge.'

'They are secret words,' said Anna. 'We will have to get a secret place ready. Wait near the steps until I call you.' After a while she came back with a black cloth. 'You must take off your shoes, and be blind-folded. I will whisper the password.'

She led me, blindfolded, through lantana tunnels in the old garden. Often I had to crawl. I heard a door creak open and was pushed into a space with a dirt floor.

Otto's voice said, 'Stranger, how old are you?'

'Seven years.'

'What is the password?'

'Jaobulon.'

'Let the veil be lifted.'

Anna took off my blindfold. We seemed to be in an old garden shed, but as I regained my sight it became a magic place. Two candles were flickering on a bench draped in black velvet. Between them lay a Bible and a carving knife. A few circles of sunlight lay on the altar. I could see the nail holes in the iron roof. Otto was wearing a red cloak from the dressing-up box, and in the shimmering darkness he looked old and strange. Anna took down from a nail a dull gold lace curtain my grandmother had given us to play with. She cloaked herself in it and became a mysterious bride. The twins stood holding hands, and said together, 'We were married to one another before we were born.' They kissed one another, and told me to kneel down.

Otto said, 'Now you will swear a most solemn oath never to reveal what you have heard and seen. You will have a new name, Eshban. It means very red.' 'It is because of your hair,' said Anna. Otto blew out one of the candles. 'Repeat the first part of the oath after me.' I said the fearful words. 'If I reveal these secrets my penalty will be: to have my left breast cut open, my heart torn therefrom, and given to the ravenous birds of the air for prey.'

'Now you will learn the first word of revenge. It is *Necum*.' Otto blew out the second candle. 'Now you will say the second part of the oath.' I repeated after him, 'If I reveal these secrets my penalty will be: to have my skull sawn asunder with a rough saw and my brains taken out.'

'Now you will learn the second word of revenge. It is *Nicum*.'

The twins made me join hands with them in the darkness so that we formed a triangle. We heard the train whistle in the distance, and Anna said, 'Let us close this lodge by the mysterious number.' Otto clapped seven times, and said, 'What remains to be done?', to which Anna replied, 'To practice virtue, shun vice, and remain in silence.' Then, in her ordinary voice, she told me to run and put my shoes on and wait for my mother at the gate. She opened the door, and I found myself in an overgrown part of the old garden. We had held the mysterious rites in a windowless tool-shed.

I had just got my shoes and socks on when my mother reached the gate, carrying the Little Man on her hip. 'You've had your shoes off,' she said crossly. 'Did you drop those orange skins? Pick them up at once.' The twins appeared, breathless and charming. 'Oh, no, we dropped the skins; we've just come to pick them up. It was our fault she took her shoes off. We're sorry. Can we nurse the Little Man? How pretty you look in your town clothes. We had lunch at your place. You have the most beautiful food. Is your hair very long when you let it down? Would baby like an orange?' They gave him my untasted orange.

As he fondled it, Anna drew her hair round his wispy hair.

'Look, you can see the veins in his little skull. Aren't they blue? Where would his brains be?'

'In the same place as yours,' said my mother tartly.

'Isn't he lovely. Can we feel his little heart?'

My mother surrendered her treasure to be played with and admired. 'I can feel his heart beating.' said Anna, looking at me with warning in her eyes.

'What did you play this afternoon?' asked my mother. I was dumb with fright. 'Go on, tell your mother,' said Otto. Anna made a sawing motion across the Little Man's head. 'We had fun,' I said wildly. 'We played lots of things. We played with the guinea-pigs.' The twins hugged and kisssed me and climbed on to the stone gateposts to see us walk home. As we passed the Bowers house I began saying under my breath, 'Necum-Nicum Necum-Nicum Necum-Nicum.' Stop muttering,' said my mother. 'Speak clearly. What did you say?' 'Nothing.' 'Answer me. I asked you what you said.' I must give some answer. 'I will not ask you again. Answer me.' I began to recite the words from the cream jug: 'Come the three corners of the world in arms—' My mother began laughing. 'Would you learn your tables if we got them put on a jug?'

At home my mother said to my grandmother, 'I hear you had those devils for lunch. Did their father come too?' My grandmother was quiet, and seemed sad. 'For a while,' she replied, and went off to do the milking.

When my father came home it was almost dark and we had lit the lamps. 'I've just seen Mrs Bowers,' he said. 'That elder boy, what's his name, Georgy. Fell off the tankstand and broke his leg. He'll be in plaster for weeks.' Necum-Nicum.

I went safely to school, but I did not see the twins again. The next week their father simply packed up and left. 'Trouble at the clinic,' said my father. 'I knew he wasn't a proper doctor,' said Granny. My mother looked at her and said, 'Perhaps he was disappointed in love.'

Where had they gone? I used to dream of the twins. They would appear in bridal finery and invite me to play, or it would be afternoon in the dream with the twins driving off in the Hudson Super Six while I ran and ran to catch them, held back by the soft heavy dust of the long street. In some dreams they would come to the bedside and stare at me. Sometimes, in a nightmare, I would be lying with my heart torn out and my head sawn asunder, trying in vain to call them.

I asked Granny, 'Is God only a word?' She replied that God was The Word. Georgy Bowers came home with crutches. Hospital had done him good, said his mother.

What do we have to protect us in our powerless childhood but magic? But there were some words I never wrote down in my book of words.

The Glass Boy

My friend Alice and I were forbidden to go any-where near the creek, but we had taken some lollies saved for a secret feast to one of our caves in the lantana, where God could not see us through the tangles. Our refuge was near a grassy hollow overhung by the creek bank, sometimes flooded but now dry. We heard voices, and looked down, unseen. What we saw astonished us.

One of our Sunday School teachers was squash-ing Poor Myrtle. He was lying right on top of her and kissing her plump dollface. He must have been tick-ling her to make her giggle so much. No doubt we would have watched to see what they did next, but Alice sneezed. Fearful of discovery we scuttled back through the lantana tunnels, past the chow's cabbage field, and in through my back fence to the orange orchard. There we lay on the grass and played at squashing, giving one another kisses flavoured with Jersey toffee. We were giggling so much we did not hear my grandmother approaching.

'Get up, you naughty rude little girls. You'll

have to be put back to First Babies. How dare you play such silly games!'

She gave us both a good smacking. Alice began to whinge. 'I'll tell my mother you smacked me.'

'When you are left for me to mind, I'll smack you when you need it.'

I was enchanted by the rhythm of this, so like 'Speak roughly to your little boy, and beat him when he sneezes.' Were there special smacking poems? Blubbering Alice gave away our secret. 'We saw Harold Rubin lying on top of Poor Myrtle.'

Where had we seen this? We got another smack for going near the creek but Granny seemed more worried than cross. The day was turning melancholy. She spoke to my father, who was chopping wood for the stove. He put down his axe and went indoors. My mother came out of the house and took Alice to be brushed and tidied and returned home. I was given my tea early and put to bed with another scolding.

That night there was a kind of meeting at our house. It was not an evening, with music and cards. Without understanding, I heard that Myrtle was four months already and that there were five or six of them. They ought to be in jail. But they were only boys, a voice said. 'If they can do *that* they're not boys,' my grandmother said.

What was *that*? The big boys teased poor simple Myrtle continually. They would give her presents and surprises which turned out, when she unwrapped them, to be a dog's turd, a fish head, a skinned frog.

Myrtle was unteachable. It was because her father had been killed in the war, right at the beginning before she was even born. The shock had been too much.

She ought to go to Wooloowin, a voice said. But my grandmother cried. 'No, no, no. Why should the Micks have her? It's not her fault. The misery of that place would kill her.' I had heard about Holy Cross. Had even, on my naughty days, been threatened with it and with what the Sisters of Mercy would do to teach me better behaviour.

One of the big girls at school said that Holy Cross had thirteen windows across the front, the Devil's number, and a pit where the nuns buried their babies in quicklime. The voices went on as I drifted into sleep. Myrtle would stay at home with a lock on the gate. My mother said she could have the clothes Little Joe had grown out of. Veronica had her midwifery and would be there when she was needed.

Veronica was everyone's favourite. She was a nurse who lived with her old great-aunt. Every morning she got up very early, washed and dressed Aunty, and put her out in the sun with her breakfast and her two sticks 'to watch the world go by.' Only the odd horse and cart went by along our dusty road, but the neighbours would look in on Aunty while Veronica was at work in a private hospital. Aunty always spoke her mind, which was sharp and savage. She told everyone that Myrtle was far better off at home than working in the steam laundry for the bloody Pats.

Veronica was beautiful, kind and sweet-smelling. One morning she came in on her way to work and said that Myrtle had a lovely boy, the finest she had ever seen. An easy birth, a perfect child. Then Veronica asked a favour. She had a special friend, and she would like to ask him down to Mitchelton on her next day off, but we knew how cantankerous Aunty was. Aunty didn't like her friend, whom Veronica had met while she was nursing his dying mother. He was clever and handsome. She hoped they would get engaged. Handsome is as handsome does, said Granny, but she invited Veronica to bring him for dinner. Big Joe would be taking my mother and Little Joe out in the sulky for a picnic. What a choice! I decided to stay with Granny and meet Veronica's friend, who was an accountant and had a University degree.

'I hear you are going to entertain Mr I Always,' said the old great-aunt next morning. What a curious name, I thought. Was his name Isaac Always? Ivan Always? Isaiah Always? 'I've told her,' continued Aunty, 'she won't get the house if she marries him. He's a mother's boy. He wants another mother.'

When the day came I helped Granny prepare the chook for Mr Always. We set the table in the sitting room instead of on the back verandah. Veronica met Mr Always at the station and brought him up our front stairs to be introduced. His name was Mr Cecil Stitt. How could Aunty have made such a mistake? We sat on the front verandah with glasses of mandarin juice. I wanted to read to Veronica from my *Children's Encyclopaedia*, but she said it would be rude, and we must make conversation. When she and Granny went in to the kitchen I made conversation with Mr Stitt.

'Dinner will soon be ready.'

'You mean lunch.'

'Did you have a pleasant journey down on the train?'

'No. I always say trains are a dirty way to travel.'

'Do you have any little girls?'

'Certainly not.'

'Any little boys?'

'Certainly not. I am not married.'

'God gave Myrtle a little boy and she's not married.'

'I always say children shouldn't speak until they are spoken to.'

'Do you keep chooks?'

'Certainly not.'

I did not think him handsome. His face was stern and tight. I began to give him my grandmother's lecture on poultry. They were good company. They gave you eggs and a nice dinner when they were too old to lay. And feather pillows. You could use them all except the head and the claws. I knew where the heart was. And the lights. And the gizzard.

Dinner was served. Granny carved some white meat for Veronica and was beginning to put dark meat on Mr Stitt's plate when he said, 'I should like some breast, please. I always prefer the breast.' I saw Granny's lips compress, but she carved him some breast. White meat for the ladies, dark meat for the gentlemen, and drumsticks for the children. Had nobody taught him? I ate carefully with my big knife and fork and saw that Mr Stitt was mashing up his dinner as if it were being prepared for Little Joe. He mashed peas into the gravy and potato into the peas and stuffing into everything. I would not have dared to do it in company. He left a lot of good food on his plate, and did not say it was delicious. When the ladies went out to wash up I resumed my lecture.

He barked at me, 'I always say having children at the table makes them bold.'

I replied boldly, 'Only babies mash their dinner.'

He insisted on leaving far too early for the train, and made Veronica go.

'He hates fowls,' I told Granny.

'Sometimes education cuts people off,' she said.

Veronica married him quietly. The great-aunt spoke her mind finally by dying just before the wedding and leaving her house to a great-nephew who sold it and gambled the money away. Myrtle's boy continued to thrive. I heard Veronica telling Granny on one of her now rare visits that Myrtle treated him like a doll and often forgot about him. Myrtle's mother reared him as she had reared Myrtle, on milk arrowroot biscuits and condensed milk. Veronica seemed thinner and sadder, though she was as beautiful and kind as ever.

Granny told my parents that Veronica was far from happy. He would not let her go to work. He made her account for every penny. He worked at home and expected her to be there when he was. Nobody called him Cecil, or Mr Stitt. It was always he, like Jehovah.

One day Granny and I were invited to dinner, which Veronica now called lunch, at her home in Ascot. The house was huge, dark and gloomy. It smelt unfriendly. Veronica had the table set for four, but he came in and asked for lunch in his study. He did not bother to talk to the visitors. I found a water-closet which fascinated me utterly, and was repeatedly pulling the handle, which had the word PULL embossed in black letters on ivory, when he appeared and said, 'I always say children should be left at home.'

A maid took away our luncheon dishes and brought us tea, and we began to talk about old times. He appeared again and asked us to talk outside, so we took our tea on to the shady verandah. I tried to roll on the lawn, but the buffalo grass was too scratchy, so I found a corner where I could hear what Veronica was telling my grandmother. She felt like a prisoner. There was nothing to do. She had an ice-chest and the laundry went out to Holy Cross and came back so starchy you had to tear it apart. He had kept his mother's house exactly as it was, and kept his mother's cranky, bossy maid, who put thing back if Veronica tried to rearrange them. 'Well, my dear,' said Granny, 'it is for better or worse. You know you're always welcome with us. You might have a child.'

'He doesn't want one. He can't abide children.'

Time passed as usual at Mitchelton, until something terrible happened. Myrtle's mother left the gate unlocked and Myrtle wandered off with her little boy. She took him down to the creek and forgot all about him. He rolled into the water and drowned. Veronica came down for the funeral, and afterwards sat with my grandmother. I was in my darkened room. That evening I was to be allowed up to listen to a new crystal set my father had built, so I had to lie down for a horrible enforced afternoon rest. I heard Veronica telling Granny how she had tried for one last time to get things right. 'We took a shack at Humpybong for a few days. I thought we might talk things out by ourselves, but he didn't want to listen. I borrowed a dinghy and went out fishing, and got a bream, not very big but enough for tea, and found a beach with lovely polished stones. I felt like a child again, and thought of that poem you taught Gwennie:

> White foam on the sea-top
> Green leaves on the tree-top
> The wind blows gay,
> Sing ho! sing hey!

'I found one stone like a heart, and one with a face, and a brown one like a perfect egg. And in the seaweed a glass buoy covered in rope. I felt it was a sort of sign that things would be better, and put everything in the fishing bucket and rowed back. But when I got to our beach he was waiting, angry because his tea was late and he'd had enough of the seaside. He said the fish was too small, and tipped everything out of the bucket. I cried and cried. I felt like a helpless child.'

She cried again. No wonder, with such treasures lost. An egg, a face and a heart. And the wonderful glass boy. I saw him, translucent green, the colour of the marbles we used to stop the jam sticking to the kettle; he had his ropes taken off and was set on the windowsill to catch the morning light. Granny was getting four o'clock, and I went in to cuddle Veronica.

'The glass boy, were his arms joined to his sides, or did they move like a doll's? Was he a baby boy or a grown-up boy? Could you stand him up like an ornament? Was he hollow or glass all through?'

'Not that kind of boy,' she said. 'Bring me your book of words.' I brought the book, and she wrote down BUOY. 'It's something that keeps you afloat in the water. Or tells you there are dangers, like rocks underneath. This one was a ball of glass, hollow inside; not a doll, my darling.'

My friend Alice was brought in that night to hear the wireless. We sat in our nightgowns with one head-phone each.

'What can you hear?' asked my father.

'A piano playing. Ladies singing.'

'What are they singing?'

Alice did not know, though we had learnt the song at school. Her family was not musical.

My father said wireless would change the world.

> *— Over the rolling waters go,*
> *Come from the dying moon and blow,*
> *Blow him again to me —*

I mourned for the green glass boy, born of a mistake in my head, floating on the waves in his net cradle as I lay before sleep listening to the stone-curlews. But I did not grieve for Myrtle's baby.

Our street was full of boys. It was nature's way of making up for the Great War.

'This Artifice of Air'

I

Dazed by your celestial height
I summon you by name: sustain me,
Father Aether, hold me firm.
Virtuoso of high clouds
come down from your solitudes,
come in your outlandish crimson,
fold me in your evening arms
safely out of tweaking reach
of tightly-buttoned Little Masters.
Let me be your golden child.
Teach me with your tongue of lightning
polynomial enchantment.
Sweet Sir Aether, set your hands
on my hipbones, here and here,
Swear at dead of night we'll lie
in one another's arms and die.

II

Nature, they often say, is ever new.
I doubt it, looking at that ancient crow,
frayed hunchback on a bushfire-blackened limb.
He'll never see the ducklings' kingdom come
though he's breakfasted on egg.
                              My death has been
promised by water in a true friend's dream.
I'll come again to shore, my bones picked clean
by seaweed-mantled crabs, and ground to grit,
dividend of the tempests underfoot
of crows maybe, or lovers, or chanticleer
to whom I'm given as shellgrit.
                              Only swear
you'll mourn me, old and dying, whip the rough
waters to a grand Wagnerian huff—
Goldenchild's Liebestod.
                              Crow takes to air.
in curdled mist his lumbering ghost cries: SWEAR

III

Father Aether and Goldenchild
        were floating side by side,
far from the land whose heavy law
        they could not long abide.
They laughed like anything to see
        the light foam on the tide.

'Phantasmagoric love, how shall
        we spend this holy day?'
said Goldenchild—'dive with the tern,
        or join in dolphin play,
or make a cloudy song to chase
        aetherial blues away?

'Or shall we spend a thoughtful hour
        talking philosophy?'
'Like any child, you talk too much.'
        (He rocked her in the sea).
'Your wits belong to Wittgenstein,
        but your body belongs to me.

'Lie quiet, lie still my Goldenchild,
        and I will sing to you,
your eyelids closed in peace, your breast
        expanding to the blue,
I have my book of Ancient Airs,
        but none of these will do.

'I'll sing that long night when we lay
        together in a dream.
and I danced at daybreak in high boots
        in tussocky greenshine-gleam.
My music at your waking fled,
        but you shall hear that theme.'

He sang. From heaven streamed an air
        so ravishing and mild
that visions lost by night, and waking
        dreams were reconciled,
and strangers in drab alien streets
        at welcoming faces smiled.

Songs of Eve II
to James Penberthy

I

Adam came in from his bird-watching,
flopped on the grass, said 'Where's my dinner?'
Get it yourself, I said, there's plenty
of everything, just go and pick it.
'What's that you're reading,' he said. I said
I've bought this set, the Book of Knowledge.
It will help me to get ahead.
Such a nice salesman. Try this apple.

2

What of that other woman
the scriptures do not name?
Cain's wife, who bore him children
could not be held to blame
for my fault, or Adam's fault,
or any fault in Cain.
So, when she bears her children,
why should she suffer pain?

3

Look how I tamed
  the unicorn
    who laid in my lap
      his fearful horn
        and now adores me
          says he's my slave
            and buys me a Porsche
              and a microwave
                and a washing machine
                  and a fan-forced oven
                    and all the symphonies
                      of Beethoven
                        on compact disc
                          and a great TV
                            and a queensized waterbed
                              just for me.

A Gypsy Tune

Szabolcska once in Paris wept
     aloud in public, in the Grand
Cafe, when a gypsy fiddler played
     a folksong of his native land.

When memory seems a field of graves,
     and youth impossibly remote,
some sobbing air will breathe to life
     pulsebeat by pulsebeat, note by note,

landscapes and lovers, fields and friends
     long lost, long dead.   Their features glow
with light so absolute you think
     they could not join the shades below.

Out of Hell

One morning when my brain was open
I heard the neurosurgeon say
'Mental events are physical events.'
They showed me Pollock's *Lucifer*.
I felt it as a linear headache.
Skeins of enamel clogged my frontal sinus.
The aluminium paint thrilled my back fillings.
'Nothing', the surgeon said. The students
dutifully echoed, 'Nothing.'
The pretty nurse said, 'Not a trace.'

They closed my head up. Now I don't
speak, but fly at dawn and dusk
with webbing in my arms and high-
frequency shrieks. The surgeon says
'Cognitive dissonance', and asks me:
'What is it like to be a bat?'

A Valentine
to Peter Bennie

Now we are old, though hardly full
of sleep, I ask the proper saint
(despatched by Claudius the Goth)
to bless you on his festival
of hearts and flowers, dear Hierophant.
I praise the fate that set us both

in Brisbane long ago, the luck
that's lasted half a century
and more, to span our separation.
Honey out of the stony rock!
I became something else thereby.
'Old age is meant for contemplation'

you said when I was young and merry
and seldom of a mind to hold
one thought of westwardly decline.
Remember me. I'll beat all airy
thinness back to solid gold
if you will be my Valentine.

Later Texts

I

She sits in the park, wishing she'd never written
about that dowdy housewife and her brood.
Better, the Memoirs of a Mad Sex-Kitten,
or a high-minded Ode to Motherhood
in common metre with a grand doxology.
'They have eaten me alive.' Did she write that?
The sonnet nestles in a new anthology
safe in its basket as a favoured cat.

She sits a while in flickering light rehearsing
the family's birthdays. 'Stop, you bloody fool!'
A young house-father with a pram is cursing
a child who's pushed another in the pool.
She helps him calm them. 'Eating you alive?
Look at me. I've lived through it. You'll survive.'

II

She practises a fugue for pure enjoyment,
the graceful C sharp major from Book One.
Friends call. 'Still at your classical employment?'
She plays it through for them. The setting sun
blazes on a brass owl, a grandchild's present.
Owls are not passerines. The claws are wrong.
They sit with drinks. She shows them an unpleasant
poison-pen letter. 'Where does this belong?'

'Why not donate it to a library?
Give the anonymous pest one taste of fame.
Make work for a detective PhD.'
They talk of absent friends, and what became
of children (middle-aged now), and the past.
Be wise, my sorrow. Evening falls at last.

III

Eloisa to Abelard

Believe me, here behind the veil all's well.
Less work, more time for reading. Writing, too.
Eventually one leaves Heartbreak Hotel.
So, how are things? I sometimes think of you,
Sweeheart, and now and then I wonder what
Topics you lecture on. Still keen on Bede?
Historia Calamitatum's not
Everyone's title. Still, it's a good read.
Expect you'll sell a few. I hope to put
Down a few thoughts in writing. About us.
I hear you're up for heresy. Appeal
To Rome, why don't you? Bernard needs the boot,
Or swatting with De Intellectibus.
Rock on, old love. I know just how you feel.

Six Odes for Public Occasions

1
On Poetry
for a Writers Festival in Melbourne

One day as I was sitting drinking
an angel, fresh from outer space,
flapped in. He said, 'I heard you thinking
of poetry and its true place.
So, while I'm down on earth recording
candidates for that all-rewarding
front seat by the celestial throne,
I thought I'd call round on my own.
I tell you frankly, hymns are boring—
the words in execrable taste,
all elegant reasoning replaced
by doubt and hope; the witless scoring
for treble, alto, tenor, bass—
I haven't got the nerve to face

'another Tabernacle Choir.
Thank you, I'd like to share your wine,
but I'm pure intellect. The fire
burns brightly, and the Mozart's fine.
I told myself, now there's an arty
old lady of the Devil's party.
She'll entertain me, and I her.
What would you like to see occur?'
—My friend, let poetry be given
its rightful place, I said, the first
among the arts. And be ye cursed
ye Philistines, and be ye driven
into the wilderness ye foul
critics, and be ye left to howl

ye Ph.Ds in desolation.
Verily, verily, I say
the Formalist Abomination
and all its heirs shall pass away.
Poetry shall prevail. No thesis
appear, that is not hacked to pieces.
I will arise and extirpate
all footnotes, saith the Muse. The State
shall grant all poets a large pension,
and lots of servants; there will be
huge annual increments, tax-free;
guaranteed honours, not to mention
compulsory attendances
at readings (all in formal dress)

by a vast populace delighting
in flashing eyes and floating hair.
The angel said, 'Who'll do the *writing*?
How will you merchants of despair,
angst, stress, neurosis, isolation
and heartbreak captivate the nation?'
—This is a thought experiment,
I told him. Look, my heaven-sent
friend, at the prospects for employment:
outlets like liquor stores will rise
 where stacks of poems, of every size
and kind, are sold for pure enjoyment:
six-packs of sonnets, ballads, odes,
villanelles, elegies—the roads

are choked with weary workers needing
refreshment, so they stop the car
on the way home, and choose their reading.
Some poets may be popular
with those who like a cheery jingle.
Others, as smoky as a single
malt, will appeal to subtler taste;
some be so weak you need them laced
with gin. Then, driving home, you listen
to the Top Ten. Here's Number Nine...
(thank God that isn't one of mine)
Number One is. Your eyelids glisten.
You think, what would become of me
if the world held no poetry?

'What do you want,' the angel queried,
'is it to have your name in lights
on every Bardland? You'd be wearied.
Although the soul's appointed rights
are, in this country, seldom proffered,
would bardic mantles, neatly goffered
in the State Laundries, be much worn?
There's more distinction in a torn
homespun than any store-bought clothing.
Poetry's private and elite.
Feed it, but keep it off the street.
Let them, whose work you read with loathing,
flourish by all means. Time will take
care of them all, make no mistake.

'Hear this, from an angelic being
who takes the grand eternal view:
poetry is a way of seeing.
Vin Buckley's written of the few
poems that are the holy spaces
in life, and nothing else replaces
the insight a good poem can give,
the healing vision, fugitive,
yet, ever after, unforgotten.
Be still, look inward, sit apart.
Try to do honour to your art.
Remember, good enough is rotten.
That's about all I have to say.
We'll meet again on Judgment Day.

'At the Last Judgment there'll be gnashing
of teeth as the unholy tribe
who lived by rhyme- and metre-bashing
and rose to fame by guile or bribe
or undue influence (editorial
or otherwise) see their memorial
morocco-bound editions burned
(endpapers too), when all unearned
approval, all unworthy prizes,
will vanish as they rightly should,
(you too, old girl, if you're no good)
in darkness at the Great Assizes.'
Farewell, I said. Thanks for your time.
I'll see my diction stays sublime.

Poetry isn't propaganda,
nor is a poem an act of will.
Though it may help us understand a
poet, it stays a mystery still.
We're caught, as Wittgenstein reminds us,
in the net of language. Language finds us
chirruping at our mother's knee,
captures us in the nursery.
Everyone's called, but few are chosen
to wrestle, from our common speech,
the brightness of the word, to reach
the life that lies beyond our frozen
habits of thought, to show with love
much that can not be spoken of.

2

Little Buttercup's Picture Book

for the Christmas party of the Children's
Book Council of Tasmania, 1987

Thank you for this kind invitation
to supper. It's a pleasant thing
to speak to friends; an indication
that, as a poet, I should sing.
What could be easier or sweeter
for one whose mind was tuned to metre
in infancy by those who took
from the closed mystery of a book
enchanting words and rhymes that charmed me
while they were busy round the house;
the ageless songs of Puss and Mouse,
Goose, Pig and Ladybird disarmed me
in tantrums, helped me down the dregs
of my rice pudding, kept my legs

walking when I was tired and grizzly
on the long road from shop to home,
or kept me happy on a drizzly
cold afternoon. O honeycomb
of unforgotten rhythms, keeping
the gold of morning light, the sleeping
sweetness of language lost in loud
unwanted messages that cloud
our ears and minds in public places.
Mother, grandmother, grandchild sing
where memory restores the ring
of roses and beloved faces.
There came an end to Paradise.
Unwillingly each day I'd rise

and walk sulking to school, my prison.
I learned to pray, thought prayer a spell
for binding elves and fairies risen
from toadstool feasts to hear me tell
my wishes, hasten at my bidding
to burn the school down, thereby ridding
my world of misery. I'd learned
to read. Enough. I felt I'd earned
the right to spend my whole life reading.
If Paradise could be regained
it would be instantly attained
when I could sit alone, unheeding,
lost in a story. Shall we look
at Little Buttercup's Picture Book?

This volume, which survived the craving
of infant fingers to deface
or tear the splendid wood engraving
was nightly taken from its place
in the glass-fronted bookcase, tendered
as a reward to be surrendered
at bedtime. By the lamp I read
verses that linger in my head
sixty years on, and in the corners
of memory still in nightmare see
some pictures that looked back at me:
not sweet-faced Boy Blues or Jack Horners
but marginal silhouettes and small
horrors I'd rather not recall.

A little girl on tiptoe straining
towards a meathook in the ceiling (why?);
a dog chained without hope of gaining
his waterdish; foxes that try
to pull a living goose to pieces;
a woven basket that releases
kittens no hand would dare to pat.
Harold at Hastings tearing at
the arrow grounded in his socket
jests 'O my eye!' A cripple sits
burning his wooden legs and gets
his warmth therefrom. A poacher's pocket
bulges, revealing the obscene
neck and head of a goose between

his thighs. The book, in my possession
still, in its coat of blue and gold,
shrieks of Victorian obsession
with what's well-known, but can't be told.
Unlike our moralistic Readers,
those class-thumbed, elevating kneaders
of lightly-leavened common dough.
Their influence was sure, though slow,
on me at least. No smart newfangled
philosophy can quite get through
to change my habits. I must do
things the right way: put stamps right-angled
on envelopes; accrue no debt;
wake at first light; prepare to get

straight out of bed. Not fidget. Never
keep others waiting. Never leap
without first looking. (Gripped by fever
or flu I'll rise and wash that heap
of dishes, finish off the cleaning.)
Breathe through my nostrils. Watch my meaning.
Write clearly. Heed the aspirate.
Leave just a little on my plate
for Mr Manners (friends, I've wasted
good food on him.) I wish I could
be mad and selfish. It's no good.
What I read I believed. I tasted
the plain bread of the word, and still
rise early and pay every bill.

Which may be why I love the gory
tales of the Brothers Grimm, that pair
who manage to disguise, in story,
the underworld, the ills we share.
No teachers, clergymen, or chartered
accountants figure. Safety's bartered
for three wild wishes. Fairies change
the bright and glorious into strange
amphibians. Kith and kin turn vicious
under the crazy moral code
where tricksters prosper on the road
to royal advancement, and malicious
spinsters strike a whole household dumb
just for the pricking of a thumb.

If I may quote from Cardinal Newman:
In art, the very excellence
of character may seem inhuman.
Bless the dear man, that makes good sense.
As he'd agree, Eve bit the apple
and left her progeny to grapple
with every consequence of it.
Praise be to Lucifer, she bit!
If every moral proposition
must be a necessary truth
then we're all Platonists, forsooth.
But each has his own definition.
I jest, like Pilate, but I think
much truth has dried along with ink.

So how much better, then, than clapping
your vision to a flickering screen
where Zombies, Zoons and Zarks are zapping
the world out in a witless scene
it is to sit, incline the head to
a book; or, better still, be read to,
and, without thought of learning, learn
what themes, what metaphors return,
timeless, mysterious and insightful
of our long quest for happiness;
of ugliness and pain that bless
our lives, embraced; learn the delightful
power of the word in prose or rhyme
to charm us.

Once upon a time......

3

On Books

to the Tasmanian branch of the
National Book Council, April 1990

As the hymn says, a thousand ages
can vanish like an evening gone.
Time takes away the saints and sages,
the sinners too. We travel on
with time itself, awake or sleeping,
knowing we have no means of keeping
from time one single night or day.
But some things time can't take away:
our language, our imagination.
A world beyond the fugitive
world we must lose can wake and live
for this and any generation.
It's there: you only have to look
inside the cover of a book.

Books have their life: you leave them lying
at night in their accustomed place,
then find that they've been multiplying—
no bookshelf has sufficient space.
Leave an unwanted book behind you—
useless! It travels back to find you.
Sometimes in trouble or despair
you look for solace, and it's there:
the book you need is right before you,
and opens up as if it knew
what it was meant to offer you.
A book can comfort and restore you,
but need one just to prove you're right
and it will linger out of sight.

An infant in my cradle, beaming
at Farmyard Friends, — just yesterday
it seems — I saw the magic gleaming
from books, and still they light my way.
Though I don't want to sound alarmist
I've hear the stern words of the psalmist
and soon will have a birthday when
I reach the dread three score and ten.
Pray that my goose-quill find employment.
As long as I have wits and eyes
may I record the things I prize.
And for this time of pure enjoyment,
this luncheon in the Albert Hall,
my hosts, my friends, I thank you all.

4
On History
to the Tasmanian Historical Research
Association September 1991

Wittgenstein, austere and lonely,
said, 'What is history to me?'
adding 'Mine is the first and only
world.' Did he think that history
sat waiting by his wicker basket
for little Ludwig to unmask it?
'Out, history, out! Vacate my place!
I'm everything that is the case.
Remember to be silent when a
philosopher has words to say.'
But history never goes away.
It lurked in Cambridge or Vienna
observing 'You belong to me.'
So do we all: posterity

is what *we were to be*. The tenses
of English let us make some strange
assertions: all that greets the senses
we sort and sift and rearrange.
Things have been past, and will be future.
The present moment like a suture
holds time together. What's to come
will be the past. The Fall of Rome
was in the future for long ages.
Sometimes the time seems out of joint,
but we can find a starting point
in any good historian's pages.
and grasp, before our light is spent,
our place in the environment.

The one word *history* means writing
and what the written word records.
In childhood nothing's more exciting
than armies with their shining swords,
the Mariners of England sweeping
her foes away, great heroes sleeping
in foreign fields, and all the blood
that history spilt to do us good.
If history spilt it, who can blame us?
Take the third-person point of view,
simply observe what others do,
accept that institutions frame us,
remove all values, be resigned
to the huge folly of mankind.

Half Marx to that. We learn by knowing
the scope of human love and pain.
We go where we should go by *going*.
We have a deep ingenerate grain
not bent by any Legislature,
part of ourselves, our human nature.
Pilate's old question, 'What is truth?'
was not asked in a polling booth.
Historians' demythologising
accounts of human happenings
must in the long run deal with things
as well as concepts, the surprising
legacy of those long dead
waiting to be interpreted.

So, while philosophers are striving
to make sense of the stream of time
historians seize the real surviving
evidence, comic or sublime,
and offer us the satisfaction
of learning mankind's interaction
with what is given to us on earth:
this world, that's there before our birth
and will be after we've departed,
leaving some record of our acts,
our language and our artefacts.
We matter. Why be heavy-hearted?
Look back, and let the past recall
the wonder that we're here at all.

Think of a ruined gravestone leaning
half buried in the feathery grass.
Whose life was this? What gave it meaning?
Think too of what has come to pass
in this, the age of worst affliction,
beyond the scope of art, or fiction.
In one sense Wittgenstein was right:
each child wakes to creation's light,
a little space, a world where heaven
lies round us, quick to captivate.
But lateness follows; soon or late
we learn what history has given:
the magic made to hold us fast
in the enchantment of the past.

Is there intelligence around us
persisting in the quantum gaps?
If so, it's left us where it found us.
I'll let this speculation lapse.
I'd rather have piece of oral
history, or pursue the quarrel
between great kings. Who wants a quark?
Give me a piece of Noah's Ark,
a coin, a shard, some red-hot letters
preserved by accident, a speech
or sermon with the power to reach
imprisoned minds and break their fetters,
a paper that evokes a place
where history showed its human face.

5

In Praise of Food

for a debate at the Salamanca Writers
Weekend, November 1993

Most earthly loves are evanescent
as I've lived long enough to know.
The love of food is incandescent,
it gives a warm internal glow.
The clutch of circumstance can't dim it.
O what a privilege to hymn it!
The fateless infant breathes and cries.
The world's a merciless surprise:
the noise, the people, harsh light blazing,
and then the sheer beatitude
of life's abiding pleasure: food.
So this is Mother! How amazing,
she loves me too, dear heaven-sent
source of my earthly nourishment.

Then there's the age of teeth and weaning.
Just grasp the nipple. Have a go
at biting. Mother! What's the meaning
of this? You slap me, and say *no*.
I'll say it back. I loved you dearly
once, but I love my food sincerely.
I'll taste all substances in turn
and find what's edible, and learn
the hard way what is most delicious,
what's sweet, what's sour, what I like best,
and rudely spit out all the rest.
I won't care whether it's nutritious;
I'll turn the cupboard out, and feed
on everything I think I need.

Then there's the schoolboy with his shining
face as he cops the TV ads.
What wonders there! They set him whining
for food far stranger than his Dad's.
He has to have it. All his friends do.
Poor mother, making odds and ends do,
surrenders, and they hit the track
for cheesy poppers and Big Mac.
I recall Boys' Own comics showing
lads with the best of British luck
receiving hampers labelled TUCK
while sudden friends with faces glowing
anticipate the feast they'll make
of sardines, toffee and plum cake.

And as for lovers, when they greet you
it's reassuring if they sigh
'you look so good that I could eat you'
and take you out to dine, and try
a bite-by-bite sophisticated
seduction among silver-plated
dishes of things you can't afford.
What can you say but 'Praise the Lord
and pass the caviar.' Love can falter;
but of those nights I tell you straight
I loved most what was on my plate,
and whether it was Dirk or Walter
or Cyril paying for it all
I find I simply can't recall.

Think of the lovesick Porhpyro plucking
an ancient ditty from the lute
hoping to set his true-love sucking
at jellies and imported fruit.
St Agnes Eve. The night was chilly.
The fancy banquet sounds quite silly,
delicious, but, alas, ill-timed:
at that hour, all the windows rimed
with hoarfrost, and a storm impending.
Those lustrous salvers! What a waste.
Not even time to sit and taste
the lucent syrop. What an ending.
I would have said, Goodnight, sweet prince,
I'll stay here with the candied quince.

Forget all boring, pegagogic
talk of what's good for you, have done
with that and celebrate the logic
of this: the world and life are one.
It's true that there is no sincerer
love than a love of food, no dearer
place than this planet with its wealth
of creatures giving life and health
to those who eat them. We're omnivorous.
Sparrows and apples have to fall.
That's how the world is. Let us all
eat what is offered. Lord deliver us
from greed and pride and all pretense
that this is not a world of sense.

Preserve us from indifferent cooking
by those who have no love of food,
who never spend a moment looking
with firm desire, in solitude,
at the great marvels earth produces,
its grains and nuts and oils and juices,
its fowls, its fish, its eggs, its meat,
reflecting that the food we eat
is what we will be: living tissue
that paints and chisels, writes and sings
the splendour of substantial things
and immaterial thoughts that issue
as if from some angelic birth
but are in fact the fruits of earth.

Think of the hosts of Israel taking
their time along the desert way.
Someone's worked out that they were making
progress at forty yards a day.
It's said there was no feeble person
among them, yet they put the curse on
Moses. They'd rather be enslaved
than suffer hunger and be saved.
God loved them, so he sent them manna.
Were they happy? They were not.
Fleshpots of Egypt were the shot.
The poor Almighty had to plan a
surfeit of quail to ease their lust.
The birds fell round them thick as dust.

Think of the marriage feast at Cana
that miracle of plenitude.
No one need ever now explain a
preference for good wine with food.
All thanks be to the grape's creator,
and to the authorised translator
who wrote 'wine maketh glad the heart'.
Reflect too on the noble part
played by the humble loaves and fishes.
The Blessed One might well have said
'Be ye not hungry,' but instead
he gave the multitude nutritious
seafood and bread, which strengtheneth
man's heart as the scripture plainly saith.

If you think there's a love sincerer
in this world than the love of food
then you can make your thinking clearer.
Shut yourself in, for your own good,
without food, but with other pleasures,
your entertainments and your treasures,
mistresses, lovers, what you will,
the great books of the world to fill
your shelves, CDs, a television;
within a week I'll bet you that
you'll be prepared to eat the cat.
You'll greet me with a new decision:
to speak for the affirmative.
But I'll be generous. Eat, and live.

6
Syntax of the Mind
on receiving an honorary Doctorate of Letters from
the University of Tasmania, April 16, 1988

Good morning. On this great occasion
I'll offer an address in verse,
a form I use without persuasion,
being none too eager to rehearse
like a bored child at catechism
beliefs uncoloured by the prism
of personal experience.
Somehow a prose talk made no sense.
Pentameters are easy going.
Unrhymed, they fit the cadences
of common speech. A little stress
this way, or that, and they start flowing.
But boredom easily sets in
if there's no action to begin,

no cut, no thrust, no rapier gleaming,
no sword, no poison in the cup,
no gates being forced, no villain scheming,
no 'Peal of ordnance. Drums strike up!'
The possibility of gracing
pentameter with rhyme, embracing
couplets or quatrains, held a great
appeal. The Muse, arriving late
as usual, snarled 'Who wants pentameter?
These days the taste is more for white
than heavy red, so keep it light.
Recast the whole thing in tetrameter.
Use a clear bottle, keep it cold
and sparkling, let the vintage hold

some effervescence, some potential
for keeping listeners awake
on Saturday morning. The sequential
blending of form and rhyme will make
some ears prick up. I'll leave you to it.
You have the technique. You can do it.'
So there's no elevating speech
on matters quite beyond my reach.
It's useless to pretend to learning
I haven't got, though I admit
I cultivate what native wit
I have in discourse with discerning
friends — and I see a few at hand —
who read what I can't understand.

I'm here because I'm good at writing
Even in infancy I found
the brightness of the word exciting.
My grandmother would take me round
to hear great Presbyterian preachers.
They proved, in fact, my earliest teachers.
Uncomprehendingly I prized
the splendours of the Authorised
Version; loved 'Hath the rain a father?'
'Who hath sent out the wild ass free?'
admired the grand authority
of 'I AM THAT I AM', would rather
act stories of a vengeful God
than nurse my dolls. I was thought odd

by those who found me sacrificing
to Moloch an unwanted tribe
of kewpies. Really I was dicing
for credit, hoping I could bribe
or somehow influence unduly —
one of the devil's party, truly —
dark angels hurtling through the void
with a small gift of celluloid. . .
An early teacher of good grammar
was Frederick Bennett, of Toowong
State School. He didn't care for song.
He wrote a textbook, was the crammer
of other teachers' blackboards, feared
by every class when he appeared.

'Good morning, Headmaster,' Kept standing
to improve out posture, we stayed still
while he erased the board; demanding
a virgin box of chalk, he'd fill
the whole space with unnerving questions.
Our teacher dared make no suggestions.
Fred bade us sit and write; he'd stage
moments of quite impressive rage
at some poor infant's bowed confession
of ignorance of the dative case,
illative clauses, or the place
of commas in a long procession
of adjectives, or the strict laws
pertaining to the adverb-clause.

For Fred, if poetry existed,
it wasn't there to give us joy.
When parts of speech were duly listed
we were instructed to employ
our time in numbering and scanning,
extracting similes, and planning
a paraphrase or summary
of what we thought the poem might be
about; then parsing and analysis:
what lines and boxes graced the board!
'The pen is mightier than the sword'
was quite enough to cause paralysis
in pens whose owners could not state
divisions of the predicate.

No one was spared. At random chosen
from forty-odd, a child might stand
for many a racking minute, frozen
before the blackboard, chalk in hand,
quite unequipped to cope with tenses,
or plurals used in special senses,
or gerunds with the genitive.
Not I. I loved it all. Could give
with perspicuity of diction
the answers Fred was looking for,
figures of rhetoric, and more.
This naturally caused some friction,
and after sitting down I'd get
well thumped for being Teacher's Pet.

So, on to adolescence, feeling
'the madness roving in the blood';
new loves that set the senses reeling,
then the inevitable thud
when Pegasus refused the bridle,
or some revered, bewhiskered idol
went toppling. O the heady taste
of new ideas gulped down in haste! —
Joyce, Eliot, Proust, the mighty Russians,
Berg, Bartok, Schoenberg, Beckmann, Klee
— the wind has blown so much away,
but never those late-night discussions
on literature and life and art
with lively friends close to my heart.

All asking, 'What is truth?' like Jesting
Pilate, we talked the night away,
disputing, arguing, contesting
the wisdom that had come our way,
caught in the net of language, planning
our future glorious world-spanning
schemes for the family of man
(excluding always from our plan
those kindly parents who advised us
to get more sleep, all philistines,
all who exhibited the signs
of bourgeois values, criticised us,
or dared to hint we might not be
the saviours of humanity).

As guileless as the fruit-bats swarming
at dusk to raid the mango crop,
I walked the town or sat reforming
the world in Basil's Coffee Shop,
self-centred, puzzled, altruistic,
iconoclastic and artistic,
like Wrestling Jacob set to fight
for blessing that was mine by right.
Stars close enough to lay a hand on
glittered in warm sub-tropic air.
It was a place and time to share
those visions I could not abandon
nor realise; they still unfold
and haunt me in antarctic cold.

War changed our easy-going city
into a rowdy garrison town.
Death, never elegant or witty,
came univited and sat down
in the wrong place, and stayed forever.
Farewell to Brisbane. Time to sever
my ties with dilettante life.
Now I'm a lawful wedded wife,
not merely someone's headstrong daughter.
I am in Hobart, where I flew
on the doomed VHAEQ,
 a DC3 which hit Pittwater
without attaining any height.
All perished on that later flight.

There on the skyline stands St George's,
and there KEENS CURRY on the hill
above the town. The clefts and gorges
of the great mountain seem to fill
with shade too early. The cloud cover
alarms a northern sunshine-lover.
This place seems haunted. Who can guess
what waits in those chill distances?
The Bluebird Cafe seems inviting.
Asked, 'May we have the menu, please?'
'Lunch is off and afternoon tea's
 not on?' the waitress snaps. How biting
her tone to those who hope too soon
for tea on Saturday afternoon.

Forty-three years. Can we be dreaming?
Children who call Tasmania home
have children. Still the seasons streaming
with sweetness fill the honeycomb.
The feeble frame's past restoration,
but still there's time for contemplation
of problems that engaged our talk
on many a long enchanted walk
in wartime Brisbane: evolution,
truth, logic, language, how to find
if there's a syntax of the mind,
how best to make our contribution
to life, how not to put aside
that talent which is death to hide.

How strange our memories are. They waver
and change and vanish; reappear
with some forgotten scent or flavour
as if the snows of yesteryear
could be recalled for us to ski on.
But would I really like to be on
old paths going right and wrong again?
Now I approach three-score-and-ten
I think not, if the price were losing
the memories and friends I've kept;
poems written while the household slept;
the fruitful pain there's no refusing;
and, most of all, the fugitive
moments of joy the world can give.

Blessings on everyone who taught me
to use the language the right way,
whose care and dedication brought me
among the graduands today,
This unsolicited elevation
provoked familial elation:
Mother now has her own degree
unacademic though she be,
though such was never her ambition.
I'm truly honoured. Thanks to all
my friends who've come to grace the hall,
and thanks to every fine musician
who's shared his skill and time with me:
Kay, Sitsky, Cugley, Penberthy.

I can't combine a pose imperious
with a demeanour nobly bland.
I only manage to be serious
if I'm alone with work in hand.
I hope the future proves delightful
for those whose arduous, insightful
studies have earned them a degree
from this fine University.
It's good to have one Bicentennial
day of your own in which to shine.
It's good to share this day of wine
and roses. May they be perennial,
and may good conversation flow
among us as we rise and go.

A Sermon

'The way to make sense of a text is to give it a context'
Veronica Brady

Out of informing chaos, everything:
aardvark to zebra, Abelard to Zeno,
Abacus to zinc-plate, abstrips to zetalisp,

Aaron to Zog. Mostly uncatalogued
things that get on your nerves, or bite the baby,
or snap the harpstrings. God won't interfere.

As Hume observed, he well might be a spider.
In fact he's language, throned among the cherubim,
enclosing his own elementary syntax,

sole I-am-that-I-am, a thought we think
among the coloured surfaces of things
that offer us no literal understanding,

imagining a silence we must enter,
a space of pure unmediated knowledge.
Death lies between us and futurity

seeming, sometimes, 'chief good and final hope' —
ague to zona in the fragile body
built of the residue of once-bright stars.

Out come the paperbacks, papaverous
on bedside tables, or papilionaceous
in bus exchanges, bright and fluttering:

extra-terrestrial consciousness, dark matter,
polyfidelity, Utopian group living,
the universe attaining self-awareness,

metapsychology, demonic influence,
the non-material entity of particles,
black holes engulfing us, karmic survival,

greenhouse cucumbers dying of rock music
while in another greenhouse cucumbers
grow splendidly, exposed to Brahms and Schubert.

God bless you all. I mean, may language bless you.
Find a lover or a favourite friend, go walking
from the Abbey to the Zoological Gardens.

There's no statue in the stone. If you want statues
transform the stone; interpret your own life;
engage in idle talk, or walk in silence.

Sibylline vacancies do no one harm.
Good poems mean what they say, good silences
mean, if you listen, what the good poems say.

Ruskin declared that characters of beauty
are stamped on everyday familiar shapes.
Cucumber made him ill. He didn't know

such flesh responded to romantic music.
But he knew leaves and flowers and Gothic arches
and read them in a true contextual structure.

Stroll in the gardens, pause by the enclosures.
Find the small lives contained in their own time.
They have value in the world, with or without you.

Imagination tires, but nature never,
said Pascal. Though you did not make the world
you can adorn it. You can say with Zeno

that commonsense is wrong, play with infinity,
or show the murmurers Aaron's blossoming rod.
If God is language, he can turn the alphabet

backwards, and write from right to left, inscribing
Know before whom thou standest and delight us
with music we have never heard before.

'Freely they stood who stood,
and fell who fell'

The Tasmanian Peace Trust 1993 Lecture

Arms and the man I sing...so Virgil began his epic.
Men bear arms, and fight, and poets are there to sing it.

Sing, Goddess, the anger of Peleus' son, Achilles...
There would come a day when sacred Ilion perished,
but never a day to eclipse the shining dactylic hexameters.

Of man's first disobedience...another splendid beginning;
though Milton wrote in fetters, as Blake observed, of God,
and at liberty when he wrote of Satan and fallen angels,
for Milton was a true poet and one of the devil's party.

Homer to me in childhood was a true encyclopaedia.
I knew how to dress for battle, how to order a funeral feast.
I lived with the splendid heroes in a world without abstraction,
where spears pushed eyeballs out and went clean through the
                                            socket,
and heads were cut off with helmets on and lifted high

while the victor gloated and boasted of mothers and widows
weeping.
My friends came in to play with billy-carts for chariots
and kerosene-tin shields my clever father made us—
Hephaistos under the house with our treble death-shouts
round him—
back in the Golden Age we celebrated glory
with our sapling bows and spears, swift-footed and great-
hearted.

Under the house in a trunk from which we used to sneak them
were Norman Lindsay's propaganda posters for World War
One.
We called it the Great War, not envisaging another.
Germans like mad gorillas in pickelhaubes threatened
innocent wives and children. Our fathers went to shoot them
with three-o-threes and cannons, and stab them with their
bayonets.
My father had come back, but some had not, and some
had lost a leg or arm, and one man had a hook
where his hand used to be before the shell exploded.
But the Great War was over. We wore our paper flowers
on Poppy Day, and heard The Last Post, and remembered.
Hector, Achilles, Ajax, Agamemnon, Diomedes—
Patroclus, Priam, Pheidas, Sarpedon, Stentor, Nestor—
some died in the next war, and some were girls, for no one
would ever play Hector's wife or Achilles' captive mistress.
Golden lads and girls, etcetera. Remaining
among the living still, I think of those companions.

Who, now can watch or hear the news not seeing
or thinking about war? The world is full of darkness.
Death and the images of death are all about us.
As in the Iliad the black blood flows out, soaking
the dust in which men fall, life rushing from their wounds.
'No use. Here at last the gods have summoned me deathwards.'
Thus Hector, and all who live without the support of hope,
except the hope that they may not die without a struggle.
Think of Andromache calling her lovely-haired handmaidens
to draw a hot bath for Hector when he came back from the
                                        fighting,
and heard from the great bastion the noise of mourning and
                                        sorrow.

The worst moments of pain are not in war and dying,
but, in this matchless poem, in the evocation of peace:
as, on Achilles' shield, the earth and sky and water,
the sun, the waxing moon, the glittering constellations,
the brides led through a peaceful city with flaring torches,
the young men in the circle of the dance, with flutes and lyres,
the children gathering sheaves, the kind, sweet fruit of vine-
                                        yards,
the herdsmen with their dogs, the valley of glimmering
                                        sheepflocks.
Or when Hector thinks of the world of human conversation
when he rejects the thought of bargaining with Achilles,
talking to him gently like two young people together,
and they race by the washing hollows of stone where the
                                        Trojan women

116

washed their clothes to shining in the days when there was
peace.

Homer, Ovid, Isaiah: read in the original language
to Milton in his blindness; these were his favourite books.
War and metamorphosis and a promise of salvation,
read to him by his daughters until he sent them out
to learn embroidery, 'manufacture proper to women'.
Perhaps they would have preferred to stay home reading Ovid.
When Hector dies, Andromache is at home doing embroidery.
But in *Paradise Lost* it's Adam making a wreath of roses
who hears the terrible news and drops his floral arrangement,
and calls his wife 'defaced, deflowered, to death devote.'
But the infinite variations of the decasyllabic line
somehow have never made the Father and Son exciting.
It starts off well: we see the defiant Satan in hell,
superior fiend, great sultan, calling the flower of heaven
to light on the firm brimstone, erased from the book of life.

Was Blake right? are true poets all in a sense unchristened?
Surely Milton charged to the brim with immortal defiance
poured himself alive into the figure of Satan.
Indeed in his latter years, when his daughters were reading
him Homer,
he ceased to attend any church, and belonged to no communion.
God, in *Paradise Lost*, is self-conscious about his existence,
which seems a little absurd if he really was uncreated;
he sends his angels on messages just to be sure they do them;
thank God that the God of *Paradise Lost* does not exist outside it.

Like Satan that God is contained in the beauty of Milton's style.
As Keats said, it's 'a greater wonder every day.'

What is your image of peace? I would ask you all, if I could,
to offer to those gathered here a glimpse of your inmost vision.
Happy are those who have known it and felt it, however
briefly.
How can we grasp it now, with violence all around us?
Imagine a world where all are courteous and friendly,
where men have lived together in loving generations,
changing the wildness of nature to fruitfulness and beauty,
working and resting and making great works of art for the
future,
finding what's lost and mending what's broken and blessing
existence,
fearing nothing and hating nothing and doing no evil.

Imagine Milton, blind, being read to by his daughters:
Homer is put aside; they are reading from Isaiah,
'There shall come forth a rod out of the stem of Jesse...'
they read about a world of harmony and beauty
in which an ideal king shall judge with righteousness,
the sea is sheer abundance, the animal world is peaceful,
the sucking child and the weaned child are unharmed by the
serpent,
marvellous stuff: read on: but what happened to the Assyrians?
The angel of the Lord went forth and smote their camp;
two hundred thousand odd, behold they were all dead corpses.

It took five hundred years to change from storytelling
in metre, rhythm, rhyme committed to the memory,
where nature's powers were gods, and spoke aloud, to writing.
In these exciting days of literary theory
how can we imagine the impact of the alphabet?
It gave us an enormous model of abstraction,
the written word a further abstraction of the spoken,
it gave us terms and concepts for a new type of discourse.

Why did writing not give us a way of escaping old troubles,
a way of approaching our problems with logic, and finding
                              solutions?
Philosophy, love of wisdom, Philos, friend, and Sophos, wise.
Another way of construing it is to read it as *wise friends*,
the members of the early Pythagorean brotherhood.
'Blessed land of the Greeks, you house of all the heavenly,'
wrote Hölderlin, and still we turn to the patron saint of
                              philosophy,
Socrates, Plato's teacher, who taught us how to ask questions,
calm in the face of death, immortalised in the Dialogues,
'the bravest and the wisest man of all we knew in our time,'
said Plato, who gave us the image of our unenlightened
                              condition:
prisoners chained in a cave from their childhood, looking at
                              shadows,
who have not seen the just and good and beautiful in their
                              truth,
but who, having seen the unbearable light, would say with
                              Homer
'Better to be a serf than to live after this manner.'

But this is not a rehearsal of the thoughts of great philosophers
from Parmenides of Elea, the father of metaphysics,
to Wittgenstein in the trenches of World War One, contending
with the French and British and Russians and logic and
                                        propositions
and the death in an aeroplane accident of his first and only
                                        friend.
No wonder he took to a kind of Schopenhauerian mysticism,
and wrote the mysterious sentence that has haunted many a
                                        poet:
whereof one cannot speak, thereof one must be silent,
which prompted the mathematician Frank Ramsay to remark
'What you can't say, you can't say, and you can't whistle it
                                        either.'

Think of Bertrand Russell, a conscientious objector,
imprisoned, writing principles of mathematical philosophy.
He thought ethical propositions had no claim to objectivity,
but for his own moral values endured the shame and the
                                        spitting.
Russell said, 'Language comes first, and thought follows in its
                                        footsteps.'
Language is part of us, not a thing external to human life,
but a complex of skills we learn, whereby we learn to think.
In Paradise, interpretation would pose no problem.
The secrets of hearts are revealed through unmediated
                                        knowledge.
(Thank God that time has not come: I prefer to contain my
                                        own secrets.)

Augustine, to whom we owe the idea of 'original sin',
says, 'if I have spoken, I have not said what I wished to say'—
a feeling with which most poets are totally familiar.
Heaven, in *Paradise Lost* is a place where all is open,
free from the possibility of any alteration;
I prefer reading of Satan's journey through the abyss.
Under the gloss of religion the ancient furies retain their
                                        power,
and Paradise, Mohammed said, lies in the shadow of swords.

I read an account of a beaver confronted with a recording
of running water; the creature finding no leak in its dam
attempted at once to plaster the recording apparatus.
So with us and our language: sign, signal and symbol
must be a perceptible something which cannot be abstracted
from the framework of the world in which they acquire
                                        meaning.
'Only in the stream of life and thought do words have
                                        meaning.'
Suppose the original sin had not been disobedience
but cruelty. What then? What would Milton have written?

We learn to speak, unaware of the new symbolic dimension
that differentiates us from the other creatures on earth.
How can we understand ourselves without understanding
how language itself can lead us into wisdom or into folly?
The study of language is not like that of empirical science.
Without language there'd be no science or any theory whatever.
In the academic world there is nothing egalitarian—

mathematics and physics are great, sociology low on the ladder,
genetics more highly regarded, shall we say, than assertiveness
                              training.
But it wasn't the Poets' Union that gave us atomic weapons.
The behaviourists say that between what a man hears and
                              what he says
there is nothing at all. This comes of working with rats and
                              pigeons.
'The hypothesis,' says Skinner, 'that man is not free is essential
to the application of scientific method to human behaviour.'
Think of what Pavlov achieved in developing Soviet science:
he taught dogs to get things wrong, to slaver when food was
                              absent;
it did everyone good to know that dogs can be deceived.
To Homer again, to Odysseus returning to his own kingdom:
he comes to the swineherd's homestead; four fierce and
                              powerful dogs
trained by the swineherd's master hand fly to attack him.
Odysseus has the presence of mind to sit down and drop his
                              staff;
the swineherd sends them flying with shouts and a shower of
                              stones.
'Old man,' says the swineherd Eumaeus, 'that was a narrow
                              escape.
The dogs would have made short work of you, and
the blame would have fallen on me'.
Later, the two stand talking outside Odysseus' palace.
Stretched on the ground in a dungheap lies on old dog full of
                              vermin;

Argus, Odysseus old dog, pricks his ears and raises his head.
Too weak to come nearer his master, he wags his tail and flattens
his ears. Odysseus brushes a tear away and listens
as the swineherd tells of the speed and power of the dog when
he was young;
inside the palace, a banquet; outside, after nineteen years,
an old dog knows his master and succumbs to the hand of
death.
Darwin said he could not bear the suffering of the creatures.
What we share with human beings is the same thing that we
share
with all the other animals: the ability to feel pain.
Language is the basis of our consciousness and thought,
but, more than that, the basis of human civilisation;
it is the common idiom in which we think with others;
not in literature, nor scripture, but in ordinary speech
through intonation, gesture, tone, we share our daily lives.
This is what freedom truly means: that we can talk to others,
say without fear of punishment what we believe and feel,
resolve our human problems without violence or hatred.
The worst pain of all and the final humiliation,
the torturer's evil hope, is a mind torn into pieces
so the broken body lives without a mind to comprehend it.

'Geworfenheit,' wrote Heidegger, an odd word meaning
'thrown-ness.'
We are thrown into the world; we did not choose our parents,
nor had we power to choose our own historical epoch.
The nightingale that sang to Keats remains immortal;
it is art that stays to sing to passing generations,

and human hearts find confidence in archetypal songsters.

Anxiety is simply a part of our existence.

Socrates called philosophy a meditation on death.

Heidegger's greatest wonder was 'that there are things in being.'

So let us look at the living world with a kind of Socratic pleasure:

discover again and again the need for a calm and merciful vision

of what has been, and what is now, and what might be in the
                                            future;

and fight, if we must fight, for truth 'and stand among the
                                            foremost

fighters, and endure our share of the blaze of battle'.

Midwinter Rainbow
I.M. Vincent Buckley

The immortal Signified
has deconstructed light.
Adonai, Elohim,
I-am-that-I-am,
ineffable by name
and nature, hangs his sign
aloft for all to read.
How to deduce the rules
of his chromatic game?
Newton figured a path
for sunlight's deviation.
Save us from Newton's sleep,
said visionary Blake.
Read the scriptures and weep:
save us from one who makes
promises, promises
to Noah, that old soak,
and then, nine chapters on,
sits eating veal and cakes
prepared by Abraham's wife
before he torches Sodom,
just and unjust together.

I will be when and where
I will be, saith the Lord.
God, what a character!
Where could he set the rainbow
in that anterior age
when there was none to see it?

You laughed once when I told you
the luminous space between
inner and and outer rainbows
is called Alexander's Band.

Wrap me in rags of time.
You are gone to the treasures
of darkness. I remain.
Some ancient presence writes
a soft-edged covenant
beyond interpretation
on the midwinter sky.

To Music

You of the Minute Waltz and the Four Seasons,
you of the earthen flute and grand piano,
you with your immortal numbers:
the Nine, the Thirty-two, the Forty-eight;
you of the infant trying out the pitch
of its few syllables, you of the birds,
of the first cuckoo in spring, the lark ascending
to carve its empire in a thousand notes;
you of Gaudeamus and Miserere,
music, fitting yourself to any language,
at home with love and death and revolution.
Music, made of the very air we breathe,
with us from everlasting, always new,
in throats, in guts, in horsehair and wooden bellies.
Sleeping for centuries in forgotten scores,
hiding in crumhorn, shawm, theorbo, sackbut,
rattling in the tambourine, rejoicing
at the horse and his rider flung into the sea,
silent by Babel's streams, hung on the willows,
loud in national anthems, marching with bagpipes,
jogging in headphones, waiting in lifts and buses,
lurking in telephones, raging in discos
everywhere

                 nowhere without a human ear.

TETRAGRAMMATON
for Jan Sedivka

I
Yod

Springtime, a birthday, a beginning hour
of ripening years beyond threescore and ten,
rich days to welcome and farewell the sun.

Music attends you, friends come to the door
of your loved household.
                                        Images crowd in:
wind waking in the sudden rush of spring

from a dream of birds and leaves in winter twilight
a sheltering tree, its branches quick with song.
Green spears in frost-bright gardens thrusting, changing

to gold flowers welcoming the world's deep warmth.
Everywhere the springing force, the sapstream
in a fretwork of transparent leaves, exulting

in the least weed, the tall tree's luminous crown.
Honour and love attend you on this day
tuned to the piercing sharpness of new light

when the ancient music nature has by heart,
old themes on which she improvises, adding
fresh trills and flourishes, sings of beginnings,

of one man standing with his friends, his household,
like a tree drinking sunshine, in whose arms
is held the wisdom of uncounted seasons,

whose music is the unfolding fugue of spring.

II
He

Beyond all words, beyond all names
there waits immeasurable silence.
Beyond the pulse of sound exists
the wellspring, the invisible fountain
from which all notes and rhythms flow:

the not-I, the immortal Other,
the quietness where time itself
is nothing, all our untold years
of making, earning, journeying,
our birth, our death, our bitter conflicts

are less than dreams. The never-ending
quest for the self is done. We know
question and answer meaningless,
and then, beyond all symbols, peace:
the not-I.   The eternal Other.

III
Vau

Prague, Paris, London: names that keep
the light of centuries of greatness
lent you their lustre.
                              Now you wear
your own light in a younger city.
You bring your generous gifts to share
from mind to mind and hand to hand.

We are played by music, as we are
spoken by language, mouth to mouth,
and brought to life by life itself.
There's a deep grammar in the mind.
It's not our nurse's voice we hear
chiding us from the starry heavens,
but the strictness of the universe.

The forms of thought that make us human,
the great abstractions: beauty, justice;
ice-crystal, insect, Milky Way,
atoms moving as if to music.
deep ocean, evanescent foam,

share the same laws that give us freedom
to take *what is*, to improvise,
transform, transpose and modulate,
knowing what is and is not music.

When the deep ordering forces drive us
to tell our human joy and grief
we take our instruments, and tune them,
and summon more-than-mortal themes.

Picture a summer night, a city
set among sheltering hills beneath
the crowding stars, as if its lights
echoed the sky's serene abundance.

Picture the dark face of the river
reflecting light, stirred by a breath
of air, the air that shields and mantles
our being-on-earth, the crystalline
substance invisible as thought.

Picture a room in which a player
feels in his body the vast night
of space and stars weightless as air,
knows and forgets all he has learned;
becomes the music waiting there.

IV
He

Things fall, Fire burns. The world
is not one of our making.
Tempest and plague destroy
the old order, the breaking
of nations will not cease.
But still earth's word is: joy.

Look how in summer light
the energy of spring
is held aloft, becoming
a sanctuary of shade
for birdsong, insect-humming.
The world's not ours by right

until we learn to listen
to small voices that tell
in fennel-plume, grass tassel,
the mystery of renewal
in ripening change; leaf-rustle
that seems to say: forget

your self-defeating parables.
You alone have the choice
among earth's countless creatures
to live or die, but while
you live you are part of earth.
Accept. Affirm. Rejoice.

The Owl and the Pussycat Baudelaire Rock

You longed for night and the night is coming,
      the rays of the daystar fade and die,
the nightwind rises, the tide is waiting,
      and the years that are gone lean down from
           the sky.
      Baby my baby, I'll love you forever,
      when your head's burned out and your light's
           all gone,
      my eyes will find you in stony darkness.
      Baby my baby the night comes on.

Rock on, rock on till we reach that country
      where all is harmony and delight,
fragrance of amber, fathomless mirrors
      reflecting the gold and hyacinth light.
      Baby my baby I'll love you forever,
      when your brain's ground out and your
           dreams are gone
      I'll hunt you out through seas of darkness.
      Baby my baby the night comes on.

Rock on, rock on, my songs enfold you,
    the moon slides down and the water's wild,
the snowpeaks gleam on the far horizon ,
    the sun will rise like a golden child.
    You asked for night and look it is falling
    your peace is here, your sorrow is gone,
    lie at my side in the rocking darkness.
    Baby my baby, the night comes on.